SISTERS TOGETHER

LESSONS LEARNED THAT HAVE ANCHORED OUR SOULS

* * *

NANCY J. LEWIS
DEBRA WASHINGTON GOULD

Nivek & Gould Publishing Company
Fayetteville, GA 30214

Manufactured in the United States of America

3 5 7 9 10 8 6 4

Library of Congress Cataloging-Publication Data

Nancy J. Lewis and Debra Washington Gould

Sisters Together: Lessons Learned That Have Anchored Our Souls /
Nancy J. Lewis and Debra Washington Gould
A Collection of 43 Stories of Empowerment
p. cm.

Inspiration / Self Help

ISBN 0-9660306-5-6

Nivek & Gould Publishing Co.
P.O. Box 342
Fayetteville, GA 30214

SISTERS
TOGETHER

LESSONS LEARNED THAT HAVE ANCHORED OUR SOULS

Table of Contents

Table of Contents (cont'd)

Table of Contents (cont'd)

Table of Contents (cont'd)

Acknowledgements

Debra Washington Gould

*W*e give praise to the Almighty God for bringing us together and creating the idea for this book. Special thanks to Monica Pierre for planting her seed of wisdom with us to do this book. Monica, Nancy and I were at a gathering during the National Speakers Association Convention in Anaheim, California where we were discussing our second book project. Through Monica's brilliant listening skills she remarked, "What I hear from the authors is this particular approach for short stories by women; go out and just do it." We did just that, thank you, Monica. Special thanks to my friend, mentor and colleague Bruce Wilkinson for your continuous support to represent the National Speakers Association (NSA) and for bringing out the best talents and skills of local and national members affiliated with this fine association. Special thanks to Mike Marino and Noah Lewis for their friendship, wisdom and enthusiasm in inspiring talented speakers to pursue their dreams. To my wonderful parents, Herman and Gloria Washington, thank you for the gift of life. Your love is ENOUGH! Special thanks to Frances Marie Smith-Dean for being my sounding board and play little sister. To my friend and mentor,

Thelma L. Wells, a heartfelt thank you for contributing such a gracious and reflective message in the Foreword. Special thanks to my son, Joseph, always know that mother loves you, unconditionally. Special thanks to the man, Joseph Gould, Jr. for your constant encouragement and pushing your honey through. I love you forever, Mr. Joseph Gould, Jr.

This book could not have been a success or it's concept achieved without the help from so many phenomenal women contributors. Their stories are truly powerful masterpieces. They have deeply touched our hearts by contributing their valuable gifts of courage, strength, and enlightenment. They, collectively, have added new meaning to the term, sisterhood. Beautiful women in all shades of colors. A BIG thank you to Nancy J. Lewis, co-author for your brilliance, patience, understanding, calmness, resourcefulness, and "yes we can" attitude. Nancy, your networking and my persistence captured the depths of our sisterhood. Nancy, your partnering and coming together has reshaped me and afforded me the opportunity to grow, create, share, and learn while we truly had fun with this book project. Our sisterly relations is a blessing from God.

Acknowledgements

Nancy J. Lewis

I give praise to God, who is the head of my life. I thank God for giving us the vision of this great book. Special thanks to my mother, Vixie V. King, who has been a pillar of strength for me as long as I can remember. I appreciate your love, support, wisdom, and nurturing along the way. To my father, Rev. James Fincher, thank you for your love and concern. To my mentor and friend, Thelma L. Wells, thank you for being a constant source of inspiration, knowledge, and support. To my many friends that listened to me during this project, a heartfelt thank you.

This book could not have been possible without the contributions of so many outstanding women who were willing to share their stories. Your willingness to take the time to share what life has taught you shows your commitment to helping others grow. May your lives be richly blessed for your expressions of love and kindness. To you, I say THANK YOU! THANK YOU!

To my co-author, Debra Washington Gould, THANK YOU for your courage, perseverance, faith, and "can do" spirit. Debra, your

ability to organize and orchestrate this project deepened our sisterhood. I've learned so much from you as we've travelled this maiden voyage as co-authors\editors of this marvelous collection of forty-three stories of wit and wisdom called *Sisters Together*. Your dedication was a constant source of inspiration for me. I thank God our paths crossed. As we worked together, equally committed and charged with this goal, I got to know the real Debra, a sincere, ethical, and spiritual breath of fresh air who is about her Father's business in her personal and professional life. You have exemplified what *Sisters Together* is all about.

Foreword

Thelma L. Wells

*T*he power of a story to tickle your funny bone, strike a cord in your heart, move you to tears, punctuate the positive, increase your faith, encourage hope, speak peace, give instruction, and move you to action is what's contained in this book. I am convinced that *Sisters Together: Lessons Learned That Have Anchored Our Souls* is one that people should read any time, for any reason.

"Why me?" "How could this happen to me?" "What are your plans, God?" "What do you want me to do, Lord?" are a few questions that almost everyone asks at one time or the other. The writers of this book are no exception. They give answers to these questions based on their personal experiences.

The song, "No Man Is An Island" is evident throughout the book. The bottom line in many of these experiences is that God reigns sovereign in our lives. The stories prove that God the Father, the Son, and the Holy Spirit rules and determines our destiny when we allow Him to.

You will see God speak to the writers as He manages their careers, He heals, directs their conduct, comforts them through Scriptures, answers theirs prayers, and calms their fears. They prove that "Our God, is an awesome God!"

The real essence of this book is to encourage, inspire, influence persuade, impact the reader to keep the faith, hope, enjoy life, show courage, help somebody else, be strong, be wise and live life to the fullest. Readers of *Sisters Together* will be infused with a renewed determination to seek the best that life has to offer as you maintain high moral character and integrity.

However strong we are, we can never get enough encouragement. Read it. You'll grow from it.

Thelma L Wells, President
A Woman of God Ministries
Dallas, Texas

Introduction

Debra Washington Gould

Sisters Together: Lessons Learned That Have Anchored Our Souls is a book that reveals the mirror reflection of experiences that affect the lives of today's women. ***It's for men, too.*** *Sisters Together* shares everyday lessons learned experiences that are refreshing examples of character building, self renewal, achievement and spiritual guideposts that have empowered the writers to be the women they are today. We all have heard them as we find ourselves on the telling or the hearing end of a story of wit, valor or wisdom. We've heard those stories in the barber shop or hair salon, at work or at parties, sporting events, family gatherings, in civic groups or schools. *Sisters Together* captures the attention of everyday persons who are students, teachers, social workers, homemakers, professionals, ministers, or radio celebrities. The authors invited a cross section of successful women of various cultures to submit their lesson learned experience. Some, we discovered were most powerful story tellers. All were heartwarming, provocative and rich in beauty and spirit.

These stories are not exclusively for women but for all avid readers, young and old. As the readers find themselves relating to the

stories, the authors want you to know we were left spell-bound by the profound stories of each one of these incredible women. The stories are about ordinary people's experiences that anyone can relate to, because you have either been there, or witnessed some similarity in your own life. This wonderful assemblage of contributors' stories has surpassed our expectations. You will read *Sisters Together* in its entirety and return to some stories over and over again. What we truly admire about the contributors are their own uniqueness and their willingness to support our dream. That is why *Sisters Together* will be an on-going series of collectible short stories from women around the country. *Sisters Together* captures the essence of every beautiful woman in the universe. In some, the ethnicity of the writer is evident, as they share their experience from their perspective. However, the common thread of womanhood, and her bouts with the challenges of life, are what make *Sisters Together* a beautiful tapestry of written expression.

To the readers, you are invited to read these stories of loving, trusting, respecting, encouraging inspiring, teaching, mentoring, coaching, nurturing, mothering, parenting, surviving, coping, dying, growing, and caring. They will touch your soul. They will make you laugh, cry, motivate you to think about your desires, inspire you to greater success, or even give you a little knee jerk and reality check, now and then. So we hope you will enjoy reading every delightful story for we certainly had a lot of fun creating this masterpiece.

When we called upon our family members, friends, peers, and colleagues to take this journey with us, we realized they were busy people. To those who contributed we are very much appreciative of

your love and support. We are forever grateful for your valuable time. It has been an amazing experience and reinforcement that there are women who truly care for Nancy and Debra. From their expressions of love, their messages reiterated to us that we could count on them, and even those we had to give a little coaching to bring out their best, we are thankful for your gift to our readers.

My co-author Nancy J. Lewis, what a phenomenal woman. Since four years ago, she has persistently stayed after me to keep in touch and to give some serious thought to us working together. I'm so thankful for her friendship and partnering. In her, I realized quickly, that I had met my match from heaven.

> Debra Washington Gould, MS
> President,
> Debra Gould & Associates, Inc.
> New Orleans, LA

Introduction

Nancy J. Lewis

This book is about two women coming together and recognizing the power of synergy. The more we struggled to meet deadlines to move forward, the more we learned to support and trust each other. The bonding of sisterhood that took place was an awesome experience as we watched our dreams come into reality. I reflect on the moments when we wondered if we would make it, and thank God for a friend like Debra who would say strongly, "we can get through this rough spot." Thank you, Debra for your encouragement, your willingness to ask insightful questions, your ability to pay attention to detail and handle the organizational aspects of the project.

My co-author Debra Washington Gould, an incredible women. Her motto: *Persistence Beats Resistance Every Time* resounded and carried us through this project. I am so glad that four years ago our paths crossed and I continued to follow up and get to know this great woman. She has touched my life in a very special way and I am truly blessed by her friendship. Everyone should have the privilege of having such a wonderful person as part of their universe. When we open up our hearts and minds and forget about past experiences that

have hurt us, we can move forward. That is exactly what we have done. Debra, your warm spirit, compassion, and commitment to excellence was greatly appreciated. This book will inspire you to realize that no matter what challenges, obstacles, tests and trials you face in life, you have the ability to overcome them and remain victorious. Resolve to remain encouraged, keep the faith, and surround yourself with positive people. As you read this book, let go of past hurts, injustices, and excess baggage and simply forgive those who have treated you unfairly. We give all praise to our Almighty God for eliminating insecurity, fears, and anxieties about asking others for help. God delivered Thelma L. Wells to offer her spirit, love, delicate care, and guidance all the way. Thelma has been our anchor and NSA mother for over four years. What an awesome Godly woman! We know this book will help anchor your soul, as it has ours.

Nancy J. Lewis, MS, PHR
President,
Progressive Techniques, Inc.
Fayetteville, GA

How Each One Lifts Me Up
Higher and Higher

*T*he power of their words, encouragement and wisdom anchored my soul daily. Isn't it amazing how you remember those individuals who inspired, influenced and nurtured your starving soul? When we think back about the dedication of those people who gave more than just teaching to their students; your teachers, mentors, or your parents, each gave of themselves to teach life's valuable lessons to you. Today, thanks to them, some thoughtful and insightful message is reminiscent that navigates your daily movement and the decisions you make. The special people in my life certainly did just that. There are many people who have come into our lives. While we reflect on them and how they impacted life's journey, do we take time to give praise and acknowledge them, for their being the messengers of such inspiration and lasting purpose?

The special people I am talking about are those impressionable ones, whose lessons have become part of your values and personality. How true it is, that you most often remember the inspiration and positive influences in your life. When you think about your growth, rarely do we think about the negative influences. I have tried to

model my own life and govern my communication with others, from the people who inspired me.

Well, as I write this story, I am reminded of the richness and blessings derived from the teachings of God's gift, to have had special people enter my life. Boy, how I needed their help growing up. My low self-esteem during my early childhood really needed the support of others. How truly blessed we are to have other references like a Sunday school teacher, high school coaches, teachers, ministers and other mentors. Their contributions reminded you constantly, that you have the potential to believe, conceive and achieve whatever you desire. Can you think of individuals that helped develop you? Those persons who helped you see the sunshine in a day? Who listens to you sharing your dreams? Who helped you change your negative views about yourself? I bet by now, even you can count on both hands the people that helped you on your journey. Maybe now is a good time to call them or write them to just say THANK YOU. If they are no longer here on this precious earth, why don't you take a moment and pray quietly, in gratitude, for they truly have touched you in a special way. Let me tell you, or better yet, describe how these individuals lift me up.

I am thankful for my loving parents. Herman and Gloria Washington sacrificed a lot to feed, shelter and clothe their nine children. A strong woman, wife, and mother to her nine children. Mom set the tone and rules in the house. Going to school was a definite, and not a choice. My father was a man of few words but when he spoke, you got the message. The most memorable words my father shared with us all is a powerful statement that he often

imparted. The message , I later learned, was an old African proverb: "If There Is No Enemy Inside You, Then The Enemy Outside, Can Do You No Harm." No matter what challenges I have had to face, with prayers and those few powerful words, my life continues on a positive and purposeful track.

I am thankful for elders in my life, for their years of wisdom and experience cannot be found in a textbook. Their application knowledge comes from joy, happiness, and pain. When they are through telling you their story, your heart listens. To be blessed with friends like John Howard & Evelyn Williams and Edward & Virginia Riley has been a precious gift. Their teaching of marriage relationships and what it takes to give your all to make marriage life work, has been an invaluable resource. We would have discussions about beliefs, values, love, trust, and respect for each other. Do you think I have time to listen? You bet I do, and after 22 years of being happily married to my best friend, Joseph Gould, Jr., I listen.

I am thankful for my speech coach and our friendship. Dorothy Portnoy is a special lady who turned out to be more than a coach. She is like a nurturing mother, mentor, and a caring friend. She has helped me enhance my platform skills. There's an angel in each of our lives. Dorothy is a sophisticated and knowledgeable lady who refuses to let me slip up. Dorothy, my true friend, is tough and caring, rolled up into one loveable package.

I am thankful for Fannie Raphael Gould, forever. Her professional trade as a gourmet cook, you could not duplicate. My first cookbook and cooking instructions came from my mother-in-law.

The daily phone calls helped me survive the kitchen routines during the earlier years of our marriage. Talk about cooking for a man who was accustomed to fine dining, regularly! My biggest fear was cooking for my husband. Of course, he was patient and understanding. She is no longer with us on earth but, my fond thoughts of her inspiration and enthusiasm will be forever in my life.

I am thankful for Joseph Gould, III, who constantly reminds me to "keep the faith." "Mom, you're the greatest person I know." This young person was a gift from God. He teaches me how to let go. We laugh a lot together and especially when father and son are telling corny jokes around the house. They can make up stuff to just keep you laughing. I can remember Joseph's early years, when we would watch Sesame Street and the Nickelodeon channel together. How Joseph III, Joseph, Jr. and myself would fill the room with laughter. Joseph taught me how to laugh, and keep laughing.

I am thankful for Joseph Gould, Jr. because every day I hear the loving words "I love you, Debra. You are my solid rock. I have grown as a man and as a person, for the love you have given to me." He's my best friend, Christian partner, movies buddy, tennis and golf buddy, and my sounding board.

Talk about tough teachers! When I attended George Washington Carver Senior High School, there were three incredible strong African American female teachers who were inseparable. They challenged you daily to discover who you are. I didn't give much thought back then, to my own greatness or ambitions in life. "What's that?" I thought, as a young teenage girl, growing up in the Desire

Housing Project. It was the last time I ever uttered those useless words in front of my teacher, Ms. Marilyn Pierre. Mrs. Marilyn DeGrasse a.k.a. (Ms. Pierre) would place high standards and importance on self image and appearance. Ms. Pierre provided constructive criticism because she wanted to bring out the best with every young girl in her senior class. Ms. Audrey Johnson taught us the etiquette skills and how to show respect for each other and for ourselves, she was one tough cookie. Mrs. Angela Germany was another, who would never let up on you and didn't allow you to make excuses for delinquent homework. She wouldn't allow poor performance with classroom work and demanded that we produce the best test scores. Like I said, awesome women, whose examples penetrated our awareness, allowing us to think big and to see our own greatness and achievement, which lead to expanding our awareness and development.

I was truly blessed to have been taught and befriended two extraordinary men during my college life at Southern University at New Orleans. These extraordinary college professors Mr. Ernest "Dutch" Morial (former Mayor of New Orleans) and Mr. Alvin Lawson gave to their students excellent direction and guidance plus, so much more through their positive words and encouragement. They taught and demonstrated the finest qualities of leadership. They taught us above and beyond the subject matter, other principles like, how to stick together as students, and tools to prepare us to become the future leaders in Corporate America. You were never late for Ernest Dutch Morial's 8:00am Monday, Wednesday, and Friday,

Business Management class. Students waited in the hallway, well in advance, for the doors to open. His messages were powerful and reflective and his lessons moved far beyond what was in the textbook. As an African American, he repeatedly would say, "learn to come together and stick together, for as you climb the corporate ladder to success, remember to bring up your own." Mr. Morial had a profound influence on me. He always called me by my full name. He would say, "Debra Washington, you are definitely an Alpha Kappa Alpha young lady. The sorority will be hosting their reception this week. I want you to attend their reception. I have already talked and referred your name to several AKA professors on campus." I immediately asked Mr. Morial, "What did you say to them?" "I said, you're a tough-minded, objective person, a responsible person, who encourages enthusiasm among your peers. You're persuasive, and you promote a sense of belonging. You offer help and information, make things happen, take the initiative, handle conflict well, and set the tone for the classroom discussions. You keep the discussion on track, and you're a true leader. Alpha Kappa Alpha Sorority should want to have you as an active participant and take you under their wings." I remember walking over to the library and recording those traits of an effective leader. I typed those descriptive words that day, and brought them to Mr. Morial for his review and comments. He said, "That is precisely what I said." Those words have been embedded into my soul. Prior to that particular day, I never recalled anyone providing me with such thorough feedback about me. If I could recall, it was probably a positive woman like Ms. Pierre. This was one

of the few males to render such a glowing and geniune response about my personality. Of course, I often heard Mr. Joseph Gould, Jr. express those similar characteristics as well. Then, there was Mr. Alvin Lawson. A day with Professor Alvin Lawson was the ultimate experience. He would challenge you to think for yourself and then, take a stand for what you believe. "Let no man or woman break your spirit," he would say. "What I am required to teach you in this Accounting course are methods and applications. I know you can handle them. However, life has more challenges, obstacles, and barriers you will have to face. These things are what I want to prepare you for. If you believe in yourself, then just leave the rest to God, and your blessings will come."

James Wallace, who we affectionately called "Daddy Rabbit," was the best teacher, advisor, friend, and mentor any one could have. Jim had a gift of extending comfort and forming a bond with people so immediately, that his kindness and patience could calm the saddest and crying heart. In just a brief exchange, one would leave his office feeling restored. Most times, that was the shot in the arm I needed, to get you through the day. He was a man of his word. If he said "I will help you," you could count on it. Yes, the caring person teaches you how to "Pass The Baton" as well.   As a result of his counsel and friendship, I will always remember this powerful message, "My dear friend, Debra. You are smart, talented, and skillful and of course you threaten insecure people who are scared of your presence. You are a strong-willed woman. Your dynamic personality makes you a well - rounded person. Just stay focused on your goals and objectives."

I am thankful for Viola Benjamin Madison, my grandmother, who nurtured my appetite to learn and grow as she fed me the seeds of positivity and showered me with loving comfort. I was inspired by her marvelous stories and her many words of wisdom. She spent much of our time together telling me about her upbringing in Mansura, Louisiana. She told me of my family's determination to live and grow, with little more than the elements of character, hard work, faith and determination. I felt proud to be from such a talented and determined people. Because of these cherished associations, I am infused with the commitment to make a difference in my life, and to render a lasting, positive impression with everyone I come in contact with, personally and professionally. I cannot stop running the race. I must continue on this journey, which makes me try even harder to succeed in my life planning.

My lesson learned from every individual I spoke about is simply that I am blessed and thankful. As I travel this long journey and experience this precious life, I realize that I have arrived at this point in time, poised and prepared to make my contribution to the future, and be the example that is expected. I do these things in honor of those caring hearts and dynamic people, who's backs and shoulders, I now stand on. Whatever methods they used, they exhibited life's lessons to the best of their abilities, to bring out my POTENTIAL, as well as, the best in others, who were fortunate to meet them.

Debra Washington Gould, MS
New Orleans, LA

Saved My Life

*I*n junior high school, I met this elderly man from the community. In high school I grew to like and respect him. Upon graduating from high school, he bought me an expensive watch and took me out to lunch. During lunch, this man told me he liked me and respected me, and asked me to come and work for him. I told him I was sorry but, I couldn't because I would be moving out of town.

A month later, he asked me to marry him. I didn't take him seriously, until he started going into the details of all his assets, telling me how some day, it would all be mine. The offer of marriage and the probable association with a considerable amount of financial comfort was surprising and a bit tempting for this new high school graduate. Somehow, I knew in my heart that something about this proposal didn't seem right. Furthermore, I didn't feel for him in this way. Remembering back to a time when my mother once told me, "Don't you go looking for love in all the wrong places" and that "money cannot buy love or happiness."

Soon, I left town, knowing I had made the right decision in

refusing his proposal. I kept in touch. A few years later, I learned this man was ill. He telephoned and had asked to see me. Upon visiting him, we talked for awhile about old times, and he jokingly told me again, reminding me of his offer, that everything he owned could have been mine, if I had married him. I wished him well, and said I would visit him again, soon.

I never got an opportunity to see him alive again. Some months later, I learned that he had met an untimely death, and when the autopsy was performed, it was discovered that he had AIDS. This man, I was later to discover, was also gay.

Lessons Learned: I am grateful that I listened to those few words of advice, my mother once told me, "not to go looking for love in all the wrong places" and "money cannot buy love or happiness." Those words very well may have saved my life.

A.A.G.
New Orleans, LA.

Don't Look Back

"$\mathcal{D}$*o not look behind you nor stay anywhere in the plain. Escape to the mountains, lest you be destroyed." "But his wife looked back behind him, and she became a pillar of salt."*

Genesis 19:17 & 26

On My Family

My mother died of cancer when I was nineteen years old. Her death had a tremendous impact on my life and the lives of my father, brother and grandmother. I did not realize until her death that she was the rock and anchor of our family. From September 1973 until now, my family has struggled to overcome in the face of this great loss. When I look back, I think we would have been best served by family grief counseling and talking more, supportively to one another, about the impact my mother's death had on each of us.

On Friends and Myself

Even now, my friends have become my family. Through my mother's death and the number of unfortunate circumstances, my friends have been my support. Its funny that I'm now surrounded by a dozen or so individuals that I've known since fourth grade, through high school, college or graduate school. There are a few close friends

that I've worked with in various cities. Some friendships have evolved while others have faded away, as our lives have taken us in different directions.

I have just celebrated my 43rd birthday and for the past months, I have been reflecting on my life. In earlier years, I spent an inordinate amount of time in preparation for college and graduate school. I often regret the number of bad relationships I allowed myself to participate in. I have also been critical of myself because I was not financially conscious in my twenty's and thirty's. Another question I used to tarry with subjectively was, "Why didn't I get to marry and have a child in my twenty's or early thirty's?"

As I continued to reminisce about regrets of my past, I thought about this Genesis passage in the bible, "Do not look behind you, what purpose does it serve?" Well, for me I have learned one thing. Through all of my difficulties, sadness, good times and successes, God has been with me. He has provided me with the strength, courage, and wisdom to overcome all obstacles. He has brought people into my life that nurtured and supported me. But more than anything, He is carving out my life according to his Master Plan. What I have deemed as failures or mistakes, God is calling his training camp. He is continually preparing me to do His glorious work.

So, as I march towards my 50th, I'll spend less time looking back and more time preparing for what lies ahead. I'll spend more time being thankful for what God has given me and for the time spent with those who have helped me along the way.

Cynthia Curry Crim
Chicago, IL

Thank You, Nicole

*E*arly that Monday afternoon, I was sitting in the den reading the daily paper when the news article about Nicole Brown Simpson's murder captured my attention. As I read the account of her 911 phone call, the hurt surfaced and tears came to my eyes. I thought, "That was me!" But I brushed the tears aside and continued reading the remainder of the paper.

Afterwards, I turned on the television to listen to the weather report. There, coming across the T.V. was Nicole's frantic 911 phone call, her voice conveying her terror and pleading for help. Again, I thought, "That was me . . . me, making that phone call . . . me trying to get through to the police . . . me, being stopped by having the phone ripped off the wall . . . me, having this happen again!" The pain surfaced once more, and a heavy aching pierced my heart. This time, the tears erupted. I quickly turned off the television, not wanting to hear any more details. Again, I shoved aside those awful memories and went on with my day. I ate supper, went to aerobics, came home, and showered. I felt fine.

An hour later, I was speaking to my friend Brenda on the phone when my heart suddenly felt like it was going to explode. My left arm began to tingle; I became dizzy and lightheaded. Soon, my entire arm felt numb. The crushing pain in my heart deepened. Brenda suggested that I go to the hospital, but I declined, saying the pain would go away. However, the symptoms intensified. I suddenly became nauseated and felt like I had indigestion. At that point, I feared I was having a heart attack. Brenda offered to drive me to the hospital, but realizing I could get there more quickly, I asked her to meet me at the emergency room. Not once did the thought occur to me that I could have a heart attack on the way.

Fortunately, I arrived at the hospital safely and was admitted. As part of the diagnostic procedures, I underwent a stress test the next morning. The faster the treadmill moved, the quicker I increased my pace. The steeper the incline became, the more rapidly I ran. "Gosh," commented my physician, "you're not even out of breath! The treadmill is the one getting the workout instead of you. Nothing is wrong with your heart!" That stress test, as well as the other tests confirmed my doctor's suspicions. Nothing was physically wrong with me—I simply had suffered an anxiety attack.

That episode marked a turning point in my life; however, I had not yet recognized its impact. No, I didn't have a heart attack. It was anxiety. But, what was my body telling me? It was giving me a critical message - - I had not yet dealt with a major problem. I had denied to everyone, including myself, that I had been in an abusive marriage for almost thirty years. I had stuffed down all my hurt and

had not allowed myself to feel or acknowledge the pain.

I had been a great actress at covering up the abuse. I told no one; in fact, I lied to my family, my friends, my co-workers, my doctors, even myself! I didn't want anyone to know what was happening. After all, I had the "perfect family": my husband, my daughters, and I attended church together as a family every Sunday. My daughters excelled in school and we were all involved in community activities. I was an educator with many hours of study beyond a masters degree. I was an intelligent woman. This was not supposed to happen to someone like me. But it had!!!

I could no longer hide from myself, from the abuse, or from the pain. Yes, the abuse had been constant in my twenty-seven years of marriage. I had to admit it and deal with it. But what was I to do? I needed help.

While reading the daily paper the afternoon of my discharge from the hospital, I noticed that a support group was meeting that very next day at Chez Hope, an organization for victims of domestic violence. I decided to attend. My heart raced as I drove up to the quaint, little house, walked up to the front door, and knocked. I was scared to death and had no idea of what to expect, but I knew I finally was taking the initial step . . . asking for the help I needed so badly.

My fear subsided slightly as a friendly-looking counselor with a smile on her face opened the door. What I discovered that afternoon shocked me. I knew I had experienced abuse, but I had never realized the severity or its lasting effects. When the counselor questioned me about the various types of abusive behaviors to which

I had been subjected, I responded "No" to many of them when the answer really was "YES!" Even during that interview, I still unconsciously denied the extent of my abuse.

The counselor handed me a packet of information on domestic violence, and I then joined the support group meeting at the time. I listened closely to the account of one of the battered women. Nervously wiping away her tears with a tissue, she kept repeating in a frightened voice, "It's all my fault. I made him mad. That's why he beat me!" I knew that feeling well. The night my husband grabbed his leather belt and yanked it around my neck, ready to strangle me, I felt like I deserved to die!

Startled back to the present, I heard the counselor state, "No one deserves to be beaten, and no one deserves to be hit. That's not the way to handle anger." This simple statement made me realize for the first time in my life, that I had not deserved the abuse to which I had been subjected.

And, so began recovery from one of the most devastating problems a person can face - - being the victim of domestic violence. I had to admit to myself the extent of the abuse, had to face the pain, and had to work through it. I had to recognize how abuse affects its victims so I could forgive myself and realize that I never deserved to be abused. I had to learn the characteristics of an abuser and his patterns of behavior so I could stop placing myself in abusive relationships. At that point, I still had not learned how. Even though I had been divorced for almost two years, my ex-husband continued to stalk and harass me. I was out of the marriage, but I was not yet

broken free from the prison of abuse. Chez Hope provided me with the weapons I needed by arming me with a wealth of information on abuse and methods of utilizing the legal system to protect myself. That information, the support group, and the counselors at Chez Hope taught me how to create a better life for myself and to regain my identity.

Unlike Nicole Brown Simpson, my story has a happy ending. I now present workshops and seminars to help others overcome obstacles in their lives and am writing a book to let people know that they, too, can overcome their fears to create a better life. Even though Nicole's struggle ended in death, her 911 phone call helped me break free from the oppressive chains of abuse and find Carol again. Nicole helped me to regain my life.

Carol Pierce, MEd
Raceland, LA.

Friends Helping Friends

*T*his is a story about friends and their constant encouragement for your growth as an individual living your dreams. I will be forever grateful and appreciative of Melba Joshua Ferdinand and Akua Wambui (a.k.a. Carol Bebelle) for their focus, care, nurturing, and sharing information which helped me to transform my vision and to pursue my business aspirations.

It all started quite incidentally. I picked up the phone one day to say, "What are your plans for lunch today?" It was a Wednesday morning conversation that had an affect on each of our lives, forever. In fact, it was a breakthrough for Melba, Akua, and I, one that moved our relationship and friendship to a new and wonderful level. This lunch meeting every Wednesday became a tradition that lasted for a year. We would meet and talk about our personal and professional goals and how we could effectively achieve them. Our goals were more like big dreams that were far off in the future, at the time.

We rarely discussed family issues. This time was designed to give attention to preparation for dynamic growth. We were to each other, someone to listen to; someone who honestly cared. We didn't discuss office politics although we did express our disappointment in

our present jobs. Even expressing these disappointments seemed to empower us to try something new. We had to strip away layers of negative feelings and thoughts, brought on by the burden of misguided career paths. We learned how to get off it, and to stop blaming, complaining and griping about situations; especially those which we really had full control of.

We each made a decision to accept the things happening in our lives and to change those things that we could. We began by renewing our ability to reshape our attitudes and career directions. The first month was spent just dumping out and sorting those mixed messages and feelings of how and why we ended up in our present jobs. We knew we had jobs, and not careers. By the second month we reached an effective level of listening to each other. We were now ready to commit to paper a contract of commitment and confidentiality. This contract became our "credo" or mission statement as we created new realities in our lives.

The question was simply..."Where do we want to go from here?" It wasn't easy at first because there were times when the tension of the office environment distracted us from our goals and objectives. However, Wednesday became our well-spring of renewed strength. Once we arrived and greeted each other with smiles, hugs, and kisses, we focused on each others' development and charged ahead with enthusiasm and purpose. Wednesday's became my favorite day of the week. I felt safe and loved by Melba and Akua. The Columns Restaurant on St. Charles Avenue was our meeting place each week. We'd scan the menu, order our food, spend a few

minutes with small talk, and then we got down to business. We were focused and on a mission.

One hour was devoted to travel time. At this power lunch, we divided our contracted time ten minutes per person for progress and status reports of our personal or professional goals plus five minutes each for a recap. We respected our precious time together as well as each others' time to speak. We didn't comment on each others plan of action, unless asked. We were sincerely open to feedback. We maintained simple groundrules to follow and we knew that it was important to allow for each other's insecure moments, vulnerability, and fear. Through it all, we were able to just hang loose. We laughed, hugged and were vulnerable, at times. We cried and were angry when we were scared to take the risk, and disappointed when sometimes the path still wasn't clear. What came out of our meetings were lots of breakthroughs and wonderful empowering sessions every week.

The meetings filled a tremendous void, as the rest of the afternoon you were energized and feeling exhilarated. We were eager to see each other develop to the next level and provided constant coaching to assure we achieved our peak performance and desired goals. We were excited and enthusiastic when one of our ideas or goals moved us further along the way. We realized that we had to return to jobs we didn't like but we were motivated to deal with our temporary setbacks and reality.

We made up our minds to deal with what the present had to offer, at least for now. It was a temporary path in a long journey. Our jobs were our livelihood, at least for now. We were gratified that our

coming together brightened our days. It inspired each of us to test the waters. Every week we challenged ourselves to be on our word and produce the results by the next week or by the scheduled timetable. Each of us maintained our commitment and agreement with ourselves. After a year, we were ready to venture out and live our dreams.

I joined Toastmasters International and the following year the National Speakers Association. I began speaking to other Toastmasters clubs, civic organizations, schools, and universities for free. My friends knew about my incredible organizational and time management skills so I consulted with them after work hours and weekends, as a market strategy, to circulate the news that I was starting my own business.

I only shared my vision at the time, with my mother and husband. They were my biggest cheerleaders. My husband Joe is a true blessing from God. A secure man who only wants the best for me. He never blocked my growth. He encouraged me to stay focused and live out my dreams. My mother's nurturing and listening also helped me stay focused.

While I always wanted to tell my family members what I had been doing for over a year, I found myself in the first few minutes telling my victory stories then suddenly, they would cut me off. I ended up listening to their opinions about taking risks. "Who do you think you are trying to do something different? If you can do it, so can I." In a naive way, I wanted to believe that my sharing with friends and family members would actually help motivate them to

challenge their minds and live their dreams in life. Unfortunately, everyone is not on your team like a mom or a husband.

I discovered there are a lot of dreamers who never try to make their dreams come true. And unfortunately, they don't want to see you succeed either. When people ask you why must you be different, get away from those dream busters. Their mission is to discourage and block your vision. What I have learned is that, they too have dreams but are afraid to go after them with a passion. Ultimately, they want to change your direction. Luckily, mom, hubby, and friends like Melba and Akua were there for me from the beginning.

Throughout all of our meetings we were anchoring our souls. Telling it all, saying it all, saying it so loudly that those dreams turned into visions and the visions realities. Melba and Kenneth Ferdinand are the proud owners of a coffee house in New Orleans called PJ's at 634 Frenchman Street in New Orleans. Akua is also an entrepreneur. She is doing great as a consultant in grant writing and master planning. Akua also is a writer and has written several short stories. She is a published poet and a playwright, as well. Both friends once worked for the City of New Orleans. I was employed with the Regional Transit Authority. I was determined to start my business as a professional speaker, trainer and management consultant. Who would have ever thought that in 1986, a gathering at lunchtime would have launched our future careers.

What we accomplished every week could not be shared with some friends and family members. Some would go so far as to intentionally derail your excitement. We've all heard it before. "Girl,

don't you dare leave that safe job. It's too risky, Debra. Why can't you settle for being average like everybody else. You're not the only one in the family who started a business before." You see what I mean? You can't go telling everybody what street your parade is on. Especially if their dreams have not been tried and tested. This is where Melba's and Akua's friendship and networking helped and their absolute focus, and words of encouragement meant so much to me. Because they brought a level of sincerity and the ability to listen, to our friendship that often forced me to move to the next level.

Lessons Learned: The moral of this story, find yourself some trusted friends to open up to. In any endeavor, you need friends to listen, support and encourage you. Friends who will not judge you and block your growth and maturity. It's your dream. With a lot of help from my loved ones and closest friends, I was able to persist. In order for me to take my journey ahead I have had to look in the mirror and recite daily affirmations with faith in God. In life, you will find you have to reach out for help from others and I owe a great deal to my belief in God, to my husband Joe, Melba, Akua, and my mother for their encouragement.

Debra Washington Gould, MS
New Orleans, LA

"You Must Be Better
Than The Best, To Get
Half of the Rest"

When one is between eight and nine years old, in the early thirties, each day brings a new or different career choice.

My great Aunt Minnie noticed this as well as sensing a need for me to have a moment of encouragement and some challenging episodes that were designed to limit my visions of becoming someone of whom Aunt Minnie would be proud. I was seated in the living room that day, for "a little talk" about my future, especially in the job market.

The basic theme revolved around who I was and who I could become. "You Must Be Better Than the Best, To Get Half Of The Rest" was the motto she taught me that day. It matters not how you looked on the outside, but your character, values, feelings, and beliefs are what matter in the end. It was paramount to emphasize spiritual, moral, and intellectual development in addition to physical features - color of skin and length of hair, with Aunt Minnie.

It was during high school when I began to grasp the significance of Aunt Minnie's motto. Education, skills, and training

do not guarantee that one gets a job or in some instances, a solid interview. With the help of God, my family, church, teachers, friends, and strangers, my dream of becoming a contributor, and not just a consumer, was fulfilled.

Encouragement and assistance were vehicles to reaching my goals. At three score and ten, plus three years of age, I remember Aunt Minnie with gratitude and love. I also remember Micah 6:8 *"He hath showed thee, O man, what is good; and what doth the Lord require of thee, but to do justly, and to love mercy, and to walk humbly with thy God."*

Be better than the best and do everything to the glory of the giver of life — Our Heavenly Father.

Evelyn Davis Williams
Knoxville, TN

Sleepless Nights

I was born on March 10, 1964, the third eldest of ten children. My mother was a single parent for most of my childhood. This situation placed an enormous burden on me and my older sister, since my mother worked numerous odd jobs to keep the family fed. We did not live in the best surroundings. One residence, in particular, that has left a profound affect on my life was the St. Thomas Housing Project.

Growing up in the St. Thomas Housing Project was a living nightmare for a child. I could remember the constant ridicule from the other children in the neighborhood. Mother never allowed us to play outside, because of the violence in the neighborhood. Children would literally throw objects at me and my older sister as we walked toward the bus stop.

Physical and sexual abuse was a constant threat in my life. The fear of not behaving accordingly gave me many sleepless nights. One such incident caused me to loose a tooth, and my memory for three months (I was told). Recalling the incident from my memory truly saddens me. I had awakened and dressed for school as I had done many times before. After breakfast, my sister and I walked toward the bus stop, as usual. The bus was running later than usual and I decided to go into the corner store with my meager savings to purchase a snack. No sooner had I gone into the store, the bus arrived

and I missed it. Frightened to death of the consequences from my mother and crying, I started walking to school. I had no idea as to what direction the school was in, but the fear of mother's anger superseded my safety. All I could think about was the brutal beating I would get if mother knew I had missed the school bus. Beatings from my mother seemed to be endless; thus I began walking to school.

After walking for a while, a man spotted me and gave me a ride to school. Luckily it was the school's janitor. My mother was contacted and the nightmares began. She came to school with an electrical cord and whipped me in front of the entire class. In those days there were not any child protection laws being enforced to save a child from abuse. At home, the beatings continued for several weeks. One day, as my mother was beating me, I ran onto a wet kitchen floor, fell and broke my tooth. I must have hit my head pretty hard on the floor because, it was three months later before I recognized my siblings. This incident in particular has shaped me into the caring mother I am today.

I did not have any control over the physical and verbal cruelty I experienced as a child. Nonetheless, I knew in my heart there existed unconditional love and happiness because on television, and all around me, there was portrayed a different life from the one I was experiencing. Teachers introduced me to books, poetry and fairy-tales, which enlightened me to a degree that I could bear my everyday existence. My mind was now free to escape the pain whenever I wished. Now I possessed the tools that allowed me to control the horrors of my reality. Books opened up a world of surprise,

excitement, intrigue, and appreciation of difference. I excelled in school beyond my wildest expectation. I was blessed to be given caring teachers and the sky became my limit. Before long, mothers cruelty became insignificant in my life. I was headed for great things, and I knew it, as well as showed it.

After I conquered college and all its limitations, I headed for corporate America. Armed with a new husband and lots of dreams my life was just beginning. Corporate America was not kind to me and many others, but my anchor (my husband) never let me drift from my goals. After being passed over for many promotions, I ventured out with my family's blessing to become an entrepreneur. I worked long hard hours and learned much about people, devotion, and business. Ten years later, I have a successful business as well as a strong marriage. I believe my personal life is contributing significantly to my success.

Lessons Learned: No one can stop you from achieving success but you. I have danced with pity, hopelessness, despair and reality. Yet my toes are not crushed enough for me not to move on. My childhood experience of the many severe beatings has shaped me into the caring mother I am today. I am thankful for caring teachers who gave me a sense of hope and appreciation for reading. A quenchable thirst for reading anchored my soul. In addition, a strong arm support from my husband and dear friends made all the difference in the world.

Veronica Toussaint White
New Orleans, LA

The Christmas Present

I can remember being a young child of about seven years old, in Chicago Illinois on Christmas Eve. Early in the day, my dad called, saying he would be over to take me shopping for Christmas gifts. I was ELATED; OVERJOYED! "My dad is coming to pick me up!...Taking ME to shop!...WOW; what a great and wonderful thing." You see, he and mom were separated.

Glee, such as this, is only found in the midst of a litter of playing puppies or in response to an energetic inquisitive laugh at a drop of a hat 2 year old. I was elated, and just knew this Christmas was going to be special.

At Aunt Elon's house, where we were living, was a big swing out double window in the living room which faced the street. The sun was brilliantly shining through the window pane this December 24th in Chicago. It was beautiful! I sat in a chair I had moved to the center of that window. Looking out on the scene that was before me, was a true Norman Rockwell experience; bright sunshine and mounds of newly fallen snow...covering every surface. The temperature was so low that when a scant few courageous souls walked pass, one could hear the sound of the snow, crunching beneath their feet as their

smoke filled nostrils took in the brisk, cold air.

One could not have been happier than this little girl as she waited for, the confirmation of, the love of the man who's life, she so fervently wanted to be a part of. "He's coming for me!... My dad cares for me... I'm not such a bad person after all... He really does love me." These were the thoughts that raced through that little girls' mind as she waited for the epiphany of confirmation that her Dad really did love her, that she really was special, and that life really could offer good things.

"Shirley!"

"... Huh"

"Get out of that window."

"Huh?"

"GET OUT OF THAT WINDOW!"

"But, he's coming; I know he's coming."

"It's 7 o'clock. If he were coming, he would have been here by now!"

"No-o-o Auntie Elon; he's coming!"

"Shirley!"

"... Huh?"

"Didn't I tell you to get out of that window? You're going to catch a cold. It's freezing in here! CLOSE THAT WINDOW! Look at you! You're going to catch a bad cold, Chile. It's 9 o'clock at night; How long have you had this window open, looking for your Dad?"

"I....I ....don......don't know. He said he was coming. He said he was going to come and buy me a coat, and take me to get some

toys. Auntie Elon... I KNOW he's coming!"

Ever so softly Auntie Elon responded... "Shirl, if your Dad were going to come, he would have been here by now!...Please come into the kitchen and get something warm to drink?"

"Can I please wait a little longer? I'm not cold."

"Well, put this coat around you. Here, drink this hot chocolate. Just a little while longer... and then you will need to go to bed."

"Oh Charles... you're a good husband and a fine uncle for Shirley but I don't think you are going to be able to fix this for Shirley. How sad... that poor baby... she fell asleep, sitting in the window looking for her Dad. Lets put her to bed. Do you think the sweater we bought her will make her happy?"

Later that evening, as Little Shirley's mother and her friend shopped among the last minute shoppers...

"Mercy, Girl, you know we had better hurry up! ... Those kids most likely have gotten on Miss James last nerve... she's probably ready to pull her...and our... hair out!"

"Shirley, Miss James knows you by now... She knows when Christmas time comes you are going to be out here in these stores looking for every bargain.. every half price sale you can find, and that her closets... under her bed ... and every nook and cranny... is going to be filled with Christmas gifts for your children. Miss James knows you by now!'

"I guess you're right... Miss James has been babysitting for us since our children were infants...she's pretty much part of the family now...

I don't know what I would have done without her... If it had not been for Miss James' help, I don't know how I could have made it through school. Going back to school and entering college with two small children as a newly divorced person was really scary, but Miss James hung in there with me!"

"She sure did, and what about those nights she would offer to come over and sit with the children, just so you would have someone in the house with you to keep the children entertained while you studied, or had those marathon cooking sessions when you would cook all of the meals for the week in one night."

"Yep, she sure hung in there with me! You know, Mercy, I've experienced a lot in my short years and to help make sense out of it, I've read tons of books. Hopefully, I've learned enough to fulfill one of my greatest desires on earth...to be able to impart to my children that which will help them to lead healthier, more productive and happier lives in their journey on this earth. Thank God for the Miss James' of this world. They help us to remember that family are those who surround you. They cushion the bumps and support us in being all that we can be. Bloodlines matter not, whether it is Miss James hanging in there with me all these years, or the Granny who's hands bathed me and combed and braided miles and miles of hair, or Auntie Elon, who's home was always open to me." "Or my Mom, who for several weeks worked a second job at night and then without any sleep would go to her regular day job so she could have enough money to buy me a pair of much needed shoes. Or, Aunt Dorothy, who spoke softly to me, was my gentle aunt that smelled good,

encouraged me and sang to me. Then, there was Uncle Charles, who provided me with that constant strong male image and let me know that I was a valuable and worthy individual and that for the rest of my life, I could always depend on his love for me. Even my Dad, who once told me, 'Since I couldn't add anything to your life I decided to stay out of it, so as to keep from taking anything away from it.' That, for him, was an act of love. Family to me means those who come together to surround you with Love."

"Girl, lets get home and get those kids from Miss James. You have bought enough! Your children have enough Christmas gifts to last them a life time! You always over do it, at Christmas time!" With a huge grin, Shirley responded.... "I know!"

Shirley Lundy-Connor, M.Ed.
New Orleans, LA

Love Thy Neighbor
As Thyself

As the newest resident of a newly developed neighborhood, I found myself to have become friendly acquaintances with a few neighbors..

One of the neighbors enjoyed landscaping and decided to pursue it as a career. She obtained her license and started her own business.

As time passed, I was asked by her on a weekly, sometimes daily basis, "When are you gonna get your landscaping done?" I replied with my usual response "I am not sure, but when I'm ready, the job will be yours. "During this period of time, I was even offered the opportunity to make monthly payments. Eventually, her persistence stayed on my mind, so I requested a proposal and cost estimate, which I accepted, and landscaping services began.

Subsequently I was informed that an error was made with the cost estimate, with the indication that taxes were not included. I replied "That's okay, however, I don't expect to pay taxes on labor." As a result, I paid 1\2 up front with the understanding the other 1\2 to be paid at the completion of the task.

One evening, after returning home from a doctors visit, I entered my drive way, and to my amazement, was the most beautiful yard in the neighborhood. Everything was just as I wanted. I could

not believe my eyes. My yard was simply beautiful. I received so many compliments from the whole neighborhood.

Now, it was time to make the final payment, which I didn't mind, at all. I was, however, surprised to discover that the balance payment was quite different than I had expected. The taxes had not been removed, as promised, plus, some additional costs were included. I wasn't aware of them. I was told, I misunderstood. So, the tax increase was added, plus some.

I stated "I guess I really misunderstood" several times, knowing full well, I did not misunderstand, and I received the reply "Yea, you did." So, I paid the money as requested, and had her give me a 6 month warranty on the landscaping.

Well, I spoke with my husband, and of course I heard, "That's why you don't do business with your neighbor." Well, I cut that conversation short and told him " If she continues to do business like this, IT WON'T PROSPER. It will be her loss, one way or another. I am not worried about a thing."

Two days passed. I felt a little hurt, but I knew in my heart to let it go.

On the third day, as I came home from work, dark clouds started rolling in and heavy rains started falling. The raindrops got heavier and heavier as I stood in my dining room window, watching the beautiful landscaping being pounded by the rains and washed away. After the weather cleared, I called my neighbor/landscaper and said, "Come over to my house, I have something to show you." When she arrived it was agreed that the work would be redone.

Soon, the beautiful landscaping was back in place.

Another two days passed and a rain came again washing away the beautiful landscaping, leaving the roots visible, this time worse than the first. With this, I placed another phone call to my neighbor/landscaper. Well, this time the landscaper's frustration set in and I was told, "I had a warranty on the plants, but not the beds."

I replied, "You made the beds."

"Your house doesn't have gutters", she said.

I replied, "I don't want them for my style of house, and you knew that when you evaluated the job."

"You don't have enough sod in the front yard" she said.

I replied, "You knew that when you evaluated the job and said it did not matter."

"Look, just fix the landscaping and make it permanent. I paid for it and expect it to be as before, and as a permanent structure. Besides , if I hadn't given you the job, you'd have gotten mad at me any way.

Finally, the beautiful landscaping was completed with a permanent finish.

I guess the moral of this story is "IF GOD SAID IT, THAT SETTLES IT."

Patricia Crawford
Prairieville, LA

An Open Letter To My Dear Friends

Who May Not Know What To Say
As You Think Of The Death Of My Son

I am painfully aware that our society leaves little room for prolonged mourning or thoughts outside of the scope of the living. Yet, with each new day, my mind never leaves the life and death of my son, Mickarl D. Thomas, Jr. Although many of you have openly expressed your sorrow and remorse in my son's tragic accident, there are those of you who still have difficulty talking about my son now that he is dead. Our society frequently allows only a few weeks to share in a loss, and expects us to then "move on" with the business of the living. Let me tell you firsthand, it is simply not that easy! In order for me to properly "move on," I must leave a special space in my heart and mind to reflect on the precious memories of my dear son. And I think about him every single day. So, let me share with you my thoughts on how you are welcome to talk with me and others about my Mikey—or the death of any other tragic accident victim:

❖ Please don't be embarrassed by bringing up the subject of Mikey's accidental death. I will be happy to share with you exactly what happened.

❖ Unless you have also lost a child, do not say, "I understand how you feel." Most likely, you really don't. The death of a child is not like losing your mother, father or grandparents. Having lost my father in 1991, I can assure you that it is a painfully different loss. However, please feel free to tell me that you are sorry and that you care.

❖ I visit my son's grave often. It helps to comfort me.

❖ I cry every day at the mere thought of my son. Many things trigger my tears. This is normal. This is how I grieve his loss.

❖ Please share any stories with me that you may have about my Mikey. I am trying to collect them in a memorial scrapbook about his life.

❖ My son was not perfect. There are things about his life that I am just now finding out. It hurts to know about some of them; yet, it helps for me to reflect on the struggles and triumphs of his youth and adolescence.

❖ My daughters grieve differently than I do. It is still difficult for them to publicly state that their brother is "dead." This is normal. Lorna and Michelle were very close to their brother and miss him deeply. They are trying to move on with their lives as they apply themselves in college.

❖ I will be happy to speak with you about the joy of being Mikey, Michelle and Lorna's mother. They have truly been my glorious gift from God.

Carole Copeland Thomas, MBA
Woburn, MA

My Daughter's
Spiritual Healing

On November 18, 1978, I was the proud mother of 6 lb., 1oz baby girl named Taryn. Everything seemed and looked OK. After three months, her father left and we were all alone. Three months later, Taryn got sick with a cold. I took her to the doctor and she was diagnosed as having Acute Asthma. I fought this sickness for a long time. It seemed like every two weeks, when I got paid, she would get sick. I felt like I was working just to go and give the doctor my money. I believed in God and was praying that one day my daughter would be healed from her asthma. At the age of two, under daycare of Aunt Rosie Bradford, Taryn had a severe asthma attack and became unconscious. I was informed of her condition and I took her to the doctor. Her asthma attack was so severe that her body was attached with pneumonia. She overcame this sickness with medicine and prayers. Every year, around her birthday, she would become very sick with asthma, colds, ear infections, etc. My mother and I tried every home remedy we could think of, to cure her asthma.

Taryn, at the age of 13, was very sick suffering with her asthma. One Sunday morning at my church, St. Stephen A.M.E. Church, my pastor, Rev. Robert Huntley, asked if anyone wanted to be healed from their sickness. The church was getting ready to go and

fellowship with Mt. Olive A.M.E. Church in Slidell, Louisiana. I got up from the choir stand and went to the altar and told Rev. Huntley that I was tired of fighting with my daughter's asthma and wanted her to be healed. I called for Taryn to come down to the altar as I came down from the choir stand.

Taryn came to the altar and the pastor asked her if she believed God could heal her. She said yes.

Rev. Huntley took a bottle of olive oil and raised it towards heaven and prayed and asked God to bless the oil with His healing power. Rev. Huntley anointed Taryn's head with the oil and prayed that she be healed in the Name of the Father, The Son, and The Holy Ghost.

While traveling across the Causeway, on a bus to fellowship with Mt. Olive A.M.E. Church, Taryn said she felt a funny feeling that came over her body. She said it felt like something was lifted from her shoulders. Every since that Sunday, Taryn has not suffered from Asthma. She has been healed by the Power of God. Taryn is now 18 years old and continues to thank God for healing her body from Acute Asthma. Whatever your problem may be, Give it to God and he will work it out. All Things Are Possible If You Only Believe. I thank God for my pastor, Rev. Huntley, for teaching me about the power of God. He helped me to believe while helping me grow in God's grace. "Let everything that have breath Praise the Lord."
THANK YOU, JESUS!

Sandra S. Dawson
LaPlace, Louisiana

Coming Face To Face
With Self

$\mathcal{S}$isters are continually searching for love, happiness and a sense of purpose but the search often takes us to pain, hurt and distress. Could it be that we are looking in all the wrong places? I would venture to say we are; since, the key to love, happiness, and sense of purpose is locked inside you. People often tell me, "Wanda, you have a sense of presence when you walk into a room", or "Wanda you seem to have it all together." I'll let you in on a secret, it's not always together but it's getting closer and closer everyday because I believe in me. I realized a long time ago that before I could love anyone, be happy with anyone or find sense of purpose, I had to come face to face with me and be able to validate myself. You can validate yourself and fulfill your life by doing four simple things.

It is essential to come face to face with the inner woman (or man) and work your way out to the outer woman (or man). Examine yourself.

❖ Write down five things that you love most about yourself.

❖ Write down five things that you love least about yourself.

❖ Rank the five things you love about yourself on a scale from +1 to +5 with +5 being your best loved attribute.

❖ Rank the five things you don't love about yourself on scale from

-1 to a -5 with -5 being your worst loved attribute.

Being truthful about your strengths and weaknesses is the hardest thing you will have to do. In coming face to face with myself I decided that:

+5   I Love my ability to put God at the center of all that I do. I ask myself daily, would God have me do it this way?

+4   I love my ability to put my husband and children before any other commitments. Not that I don't have many other commitments, but family comes first.

+3   I love to be honest with myself and others. I strive to treat others as I would have them treat me.

+2   I love my ability to live each day to the fullest, and to turn my obstacles into challenges.

+1   I love my career and the opportunity it affords me to help someone every day of my life, in one way or the other.

Being truthful about the positive me was easier than I thought, but being truthful about the negative me was a little more difficult; particularly, since so many people think I've got it all together. But, I had to come face to face with the fact that:

-5   The thing that I love least about myself is my inability to say no. I have to learn that there is only so much I can do in any given twenty-four hour period.

-4   I have a problem with time management because I am trying to get too many things done.

-3   I don't love myself when I allow another person or situation to make my anger surface. I need to be more proactive than reactive.

-2   I don't love being an impatient person. I expect the best of me and everyone else at all times and have little tolerance for anything less.

-1   I don't love my physical self. I have used waiting until I was over thirty-five to have two children, in twenty-five and a half months, as an excuse, for far too long to justify my weight.

After facing myself, I had to develop a plan to love all of me. First, I had to realize that I am only human and everything in life is not going to be a +5; however, my goal in falling in love with myself was to make my every existence no less than a +3.

How can you say, "I can turn a-5, -4, -3, -2, -1 into a +3, +4 or +5." First, you have to believe that you can do all things through

Christ that strengthens you.   Whenever I am faced with a new challenge, I remind myself of this most powerful scripture.

You have to believe that there is no mountain too high, or valley too low, for you to conquer in your quest to create, a better you, that you can love and feel free to have others love you as you deserve to be loved. But you say, where do I find the time to love me, when every minute of everyday is filled. I say "make the time, sister. It's the beginning of a better quality of life." I made this commitment to me and while I have not turned all of my negative attributes into a +3, +4 or +5, I am well on the way to self validation and loving a new me. I am growing every day and am happier with myself. I suggest that you wake up fifteen minutes earlier everyday and go to bed fifteen minutes later every day.   Use your thirty minutes to concentrate on you, turning your negatives into positives and fortifying the things that you already love about you.

While I have never experienced self-hatred, addictions to alcohol or drugs, allowing a spouse or significant other to abuse me, I firmly believe that you can break the shackles that bind you when you fall in love with self, first. Once you know and respect you, you can end your search for love, happiness and sense of purpose and enjoy the world's best treasure, yourself. Sisters, come face to face with the new you.

Wanda Anderson Davis, Esq.
Harvey, LA

Overcoming Adversity
Through Christ

*O*n June 2, 1964 at 9:00 A.M., a nine pound baby girl was born to a truck driver by the name of Elijah Smith and a school teacher, Frances McNeal Smith. To her parents, she was the most beautiful and inspirational sight they ever saw. Her mother named her Frances Marie Smith, after her mother, to begin a legacy in the making. Her story begins like this...

I was one who was shy and quiet, growing up. I used to get picked on by the kids in the neighborhood because I was an only child and I didn't really defend myself. I used to listen to what the Sunday school teacher explained to us about the story of how Jesus said, we are to do good, to those who use us. Well, that lesson must have been written just for me because I have been through a lot of storms. But, I must say that if it was not for my strong faith in the Master and His son Jesus, I would not be the person I am today. Let me show you how important it is to have faith and to use your faith when dealing with life's adversities.

Imagine, yourself at home, playing with your son or daughter

and your husband calls you to tell you he will be home soon. Thirty minutes later, when he arrives he says, "Honey, I have something important to tell you..." Your heart starts to pound and you say to yourself, "Oh God, what has happened, now?" Then, he says, "Don't leave me!" and I responded to myself, while holding the baby, "You selfish jerk, all men do is think about themselves, first and never about the welfare of their family." Well, when he finished talking, and all the confusion from my head cleared, my husband, I learned, was suspended from his job for four months. I prayed with my husband and asked God to strengthen and guide us as a family.

Our household didn't have two incomes during the summer, only one, that was his. But, my God doesn't slumber nor does he sleep. Remember, Jesus took the fish and five loaves of bread? Well, it was a though God just took what we had financially and made it cover the entire summer months and we didn't have to change our life style. God said "He will fight our battles if we just keep still." As Christians, we don't support each other totally when things go wrong. We talk gossip about each others' problems. That's why it is important for you to hold strong to your faith. Stop placing your trust in man or woman and start building your faith in God. You will always find yourself in a struggle for what is right. People just don't care about what is right. They only care about their own greed. In the struggle, make sure you do right, because the person who does right will always win. The battle may look as though it is going to be won by someone else, but it will not. Don't be passive, speak out for what is right. Black women, stop sitting back and allowing folks to

mistreat you. Stop giving people a license to run over you because you feel as though you need a man, a job, money, and/or a friend. After my experience with my husband, I explained to him that I needed him to grow spiritually if we were going to remain a family. He evaluated himself and began to make a tremendous change in his walk with Christ. He realized that he needed to put his family first, and stop allowing the job to take control of him. Instead, he should take control of the job.

During the same year, it was as though Satan was trying to drive me out! The administrators on my job began to deal with me unfairly. The supervisors were talking out of both sides of their mouths and leaks started to occur. They didn't realize that I knew what their original intentions were for me. So they felt they could continue to run a game on me after all the hard work and time I spent building a dynamic finance program for middle and high school students in our school district.

As long as I was teaching my full load and coordinating the program, everyone was ok. But, when I began the job in 1994 and asked to be part-time in the classroom in 1997, it was though WWIII was taking place. I had rocked the boat. I had asked for too much. They even said that I didn't want to be accountable. The story every year was "we don't have enough money to fund your position." Which really means, "we don't want you to have this position or we are not committed to this program." Every year the program expanded and grew. The first year there were seven schools. The second and third year, twelve schools. Now, in this year, sixteen

schools. During the second year of the program the junior high schools had a number one ranked team in the State and the same happened for the high school during the third year. The program has serviced over 3000 students in regular, gifted, and special education classes. A mentor and I worked really hard to send 37 students and nine teachers to the New York Stock Exchange. Not once during these times that I have worked endlessly with the program has anyone sat down and sincerely said "thank you" for the hard work and effort you have put into this program to make it a success. And I didn't expect it, either. The top administrators tried to intimidate me, mentally, as well as verbally degrade me. They surrounded themselves with incompetence and specialized in micro managing. They set traps and consistently lied to me about their plans. They dealt in chaos and mess, constantly. They tried using psychology 101 on their opponents by making them the scapegoat when anything went wrong. So, I had to ask myself why? Is it because they didn't have a grasp at what was going on, so they couldn't control the program the way they saw fit? It all came down to wanting to have POWER. In most battles people fight for POWER and CONTROL. But remember, always stand for what is RIGHT. RIGHT will always win. Whenever you go into battle with someone and/or thing, stand on what's right.

I guess you've asked yourself, "Why does she keep doing this?" Well, when your students come back to visit you and you meet other students that are intrigued by what you are doing and saying, that's the joy of it all. No matter how wrong they may treat me, I

know I'm doing the right thing by the ones who need it most, the children.

You must begin now! And not later, realizing that you can overcome all adversities through Christ Jesus. God gives all of us a measure of faith. But we don't use it. We just wait on God and others to make things happen for us. That's called "SECURITY." Sometimes, you must step out there with direction from God first, and act on your faith. Stop being afraid. He will be right there.

Here are some steps I take when dealing with life's battles:

1) I thank God for giving me the Victory.

2) I ask God to direct my path and build a fence around me.

3) I continue to praise God for giving me his strength and wisdom through the battle.

4) I ask God to give me a sense of peace that will surpass all understanding.

5) I build myself up with the Word, knowing that God is not a liar and his Word will not return to me void.

Frances Marie Smith-Dean
New Orleans, LA

"The Lesson of '95
(We're all doing the best we can do.")

*I*t was one of the most difficult times of her eleven adult children's lives. Anita Wiltz James, my 77 year old mother would finally have to succumb to the cruel way that alzheimer's disease takes a loved one away from their family. How could this happen to our mother, this vibrant, intelligent and often outspoken woman? A woman who, despite her years, looked like someone in her 50's with smooth skin and silver streaked hair. It was our mother who was 5'4" tall but whose very presence was as overshadowing as the giant pecan trees that shaded her huge back yard. Our mom had a beautiful singing voice and often sang English and French songs while making breakfast early in the morning upon returning from 6:30 a.m. daily Mass. How could a matriarch who could have easily carried the title of "superwoman," even before the phrase was popular, suddenly not remember how to find her way home?

My mother worked two jobs when I was a child, when most of my friend's mothers stayed home. She drove a car long before any of my friends' mothers and handled all the business decisions and finances for our family, long before it was acceptable for a woman to do so. Mama realized the importance of making a visitor feel

welcome in her home.

She also understood the love, healing, and power that was transmitted over a plate of well-prepared food at her table that was always adorned with table linen, crystal and china. Her rice dressing, seafood okra gumbo, stuffed crab, and her own special beignets were legendary. My husband Ed always said that no one could bake a chicken like my mother, boasting that the flavor was so good, you could eat the bone. Every Sunday my mother made the best mouth watering biscuits this side of the Mississippi River. Often, this loving feat was accomplished in church attire, complete with heels and pearls as she was still dressed from 7 a.m. Mass. Stopping by for coffee and biscuits on Sunday morning after mass was another of my mother's traditions.

As masterful as she was in the kitchen, Anita James' true gift to the world was her ability to turn a single seed or young vine into a splendid garden. Mama had magical hands with flowers. She grew huge plants, rubber plants and ivy, which she placed in her car and drove to the church and placed on the altar for weekend Masses. My mother felt this was her special way of praising God. Growing flowers was her favorite past time.

How cruel it was, that my family, who grew up with such a strong woman, a capable woman, had to watch her go through the many phases and stages of such a terrible disease. How could a disease like alzheimer's take her away, years before she passed away? The person we saw before us was not our mother. Over the years, the symptoms of alzheimer's would appear, which were unmistakable.

She was given to episodes of disorientation, violence, wandering and often times, she had once again become a child. For us, it would become the hard lesson of '95.

During the last month of my mother's life, we had to come together and make decisions regarding her care, set up a vigil at the hospital and deal with the grief we were feeling; all at the same time. She had become delusional, suffered strokes and experienced paralysis related to the strokes.

Mama lost the ability to speak, became completely blind and eventually slipped into a coma. On this Easter Sunday, we weren't gathered around my mother's dining table or enjoying the beautiful flower beds that she was known for. On this holiday, we were gathered around my mother's hospital bed. During that very difficult time, and without argument or discussion, we were able to set up a system that supported each other, as we took care of our mother's needs. Under the circumstances, we were all doing the best we could do. When one person got too weary and worn out, somehow, God gave the other one the grace and the courage to step forward. Almost daily, my sister from Los Angeles phoned in, for updates and to offer love and support long distance. My brothers often visited during the day and expressed that it was really hard for them to see Mama in such a way. We accepted what each person could do, when they could do it. My family leaned on each other during this most difficult time and somehow made the best of a very, very painful situation. When seeing Mama suffer and wince with pain got to be unbearable and one needed an emotional break from the hospital rotation, relief

was assuredly given. Among the sisters there was an understanding that each could do, and did, the best they could. If anyone had to step out of rotation because they needed a break or had to take care of their own family's needs, it was understood. Often, someone took the time to prepare meals so the ones staying at the hospital had a hot meal and not just hospital cafeteria food. My aunts and uncle were on hand to offer help with the vigil and to offer emotional and prayer support. Their support was deeply appreciated.

Throughout those 31 days, it was my sister Myrtle who often said to me, "You know, we're all doing the best we can do." This phrase became our mantra, often helping us to support each other as we tried to cope with what life was sending our way.

These were some of the most difficult days of our lives and this short phrase helped me to walk through this time and to maintain calm and be at peace in the midst of the storm. Just as the flowers of spring began to bloom, God called Mama home on May 1, 1995.

Regardless if you are struggling with illness like my family did, or if you're faced with a crisis and you must come together and support each other and work together, remember the lesson of '95-- "We're all doing the best we can do." Very simply, this means that there is no need to blame, accuse, criticize or confront. This doesn't mean that you have to like what someone's "best" is. Often, you will find that during a stressful time, the "best" that our loved ones can do is very little. I have very good friends and know many people but during my mother's death, there were only a handful of close friends, that I could count on for emotional support and understanding,

especially given the fact that my husband was away at Harvard Business School. I had to remember my loved ones were doing the best they could do. I didn't like it, but, it helped me to know that. In your situation, there may be times when you might be doing more than others or you may be doing less. Give yourself a break and remember "the lesson of '95—we're all doing the best we can do." When you know this for yourself, you will understand it better for others. If there is something to be done and you have the time, talent, finances, and ability, do it, and keep in mind the "lesson of '95." Your family ordeal may involve making funeral arrangements or planning a wedding. Before you criticize someone for what they are doing or not doing, remember, that we are all doing the best that we can. Don't be so hard on yourself for what you may, or may not be able to do, to help out. This is a two-fold healing process. This way of looking at life's situations is a way of releasing yourself from anger and resentment toward someone else, and it absolves the other person of guilt, shame and blame. This is truly "the lesson of '95— we're all doing the best we can do."

Carmella Marshall
Harvey, LA

"Mirror, Mirror..."

$\mathcal{F}$or much of my life, I avoided mirrors. To be honest, I never liked the looking glass. Mirrors reveal too much. They reflect more than the presence or absence of wrinkles or laugh lines. Mirrors reflect our souls, too often battered by self-doubt, fear, and denial. The reflective glass shows the world how we feel about our lives. Unfortunately, mirrors talk too much. They spill the beans and speak a truth that we don't want to hear. The Wicked Witch asked the mirror on the wall to tell her who was the fairest of them all. She got an answer she didn't want to hear. Filled with anger and jealously, the Wicked Witch set out to ruin Snow White's life.

During the four-and-a-half years I've worked in television news at the ABC affiliate in New Orleans, I became an expert at applying my own makeup before appearing on the news set. I lined my eyes, powered my face and colored my lips without closely looking at myself in the mirror. Even in that brightly-lit makeup room, I could hide from my innerself, and convince myself that looking at myself was pure vanity. The mirror tried to tell me that it

wasn't the enemy. The mirror wanted me to trust the reflection. It constantly whispered my name, beckoning me to take a good, long look at the woman others found beautiful and enchanting. "Take a look," the mirror begged. "See the miracle that you are. See the gift that you are. Look into those enormous dark brown eyes that reflect goodness and kindness. Don't be afraid." I never did.

I spent so many years afraid. Afraid to be magnificent. Afraid to soar. Afraid to take a look in the mirror. Always uncomfortable with my looks, I shied away from compliments. I am not certain why or when my dysfunctional relationship with the mirror began. I suppose if I replayed the events of my life, I could trace it to some unkind word by a relative or school mate. Perhaps, I could follow the trail of disappointment to an insensitive teacher or adult who may have overlooked my beauty and potential, opting instead to shower another young girl with praises.

A couple of years ago, my husband and I moved into a new home. As a house warming gift, my friend Raseen, bought a beautiful full-length mirror for our bedroom. I secretly wished she hadn't. How could I continue to hide from myself if the mirror was there in the bedroom? How could I stand looking at my face and body in that mirror? I was unwilling to catch even a glimpse of what I considered to be a short, imperfect body that housed years of unwanted fat.

One afternoon, I sat in the middle of the bed, reading. I felt as if someone was watching me. I quickly looked up and saw my reflection in the mirror. I sat transfixed in the middle of the bed. I couldn't stop looking at myself. It was as if I was seeing the reflection

for the very first time. There I was — gorgeous and fabulous. I saw the soft hair, the strong arms and the figure that was often buried under loose, unflattering clothing.

I saw what others saw — a beautiful, powerful, loving woman. I saw a kind spirit, a bright smile that reassured others and encouraged the dreams of others. I saw how the years of growth, struggle and change had left me stronger, wiser and willing to share my lessons learned. I saw why others are drawn to me, often seeking my embrace. I understood why my husband cherishes me and seeks my counsel. What had taken me so long? Why was I just seeing myself for the first time?

I now believe every woman should have a full-length mirror; a mirror that we gaze into all the time. A mirror that truthfully captures our grace, power and life-changing lessons. A mirror that celebrates the mature, as well as the young. "Mirror, mirror on the wall. Who's the fairest of them all?" Women everywhere.

Monica Pierre
Harvey, LA

Finally, We Meet

It was in the sixth grade, as I recall, when my classmates saw my birth certificate and began to tease me because, on the line where my father's name should have been was the word, "unknown." This was when I began to wonder who *was* my biological father. I began to ask my mother many questions about the man called S.J. She answered all of my questions, the ones she could answer. She never told me anything bad about my father. If there was anything bad about him, she kept those comments to herself. During this time, I lived in a three bedroom house with my grandmother and I can recall a thermostat on the wall in the hallway that had the initials S.J. on it. Many times I would pass by the thermostat and read those initials and wonder where was S.J., and how exactly did he look. I wondered if I would ever see my biological father. For many years, I walked that hall, read those initials and thought about a father I did now know. Well, God truly answers prayers. In March of 1983, at the age of eighteen, I received a phone call from S.J. It was such a long awaited call that I was at a lost for words. At last I finally talked on the phone to my dad and his family, now my family. In May of that same year, I received a round trip plane ticket and a photo of my dad. I needed that photo of my dad, so that I could recognize him once I arrived in Minneapolis. This was my first plane ride and I was alone, traveling

to a strange city to meet my father and his family for the first time. Although I had not mailed a picture of myself to my dad, he did not have trouble knowing which female getting off the plane was his daughter. There were only two African-Americans on the plane, myself and a male. Once I arrived at the airport, my dad and I embraced each other and began to get acquainted. We sat in a restaurant and talked before driving to his home. "Finally, we meet," I said to him.

After talking to my dad, I realized he wanted to meet me just as much as I wanted to meet him. He told me that his life would not have been complete until he met his daughter. I'm very happy that my dad, S.J., made that phone call. Now, I have four more wonderful people that are a part of my life. You see, I never believed I was the reason for what happened between my parents. All I knew was, I had a father somewhere and I wanted to know him. There are many daughters out there who are longing for that phone call from their father. My advice is that someone has to make that first step. I'm glad my Dad did.

Tereska Bridges Washington, RN
New Orleans, LA.

My Lesson In Faith

$\mathcal{F}$or sometime, I had been having difficulty grasping the idea of faith. I mean, I had a concept of the word, heard it used in church and in school, but it was hard coming to terms with it's true meaning. To believe, when you have no reason to believe, to trust, when you have every reason in the world not to. Even today, I have a very difficult time trusting in the things that cause me great fear. But in those times, I remember a story that helps remind me that faith can move mountains.

I had just finished graduate school and really needed a new job. My growth on my job was stunted. I had learned all I could possibly learn, there were no further promotions available and there were no raises in sight; in fact, the agency had been having financial problems and had not paid us in seven months. Yes, our boss gave us what he could, but it did not cover the bills that had started to mount.

It would have been easy for me to walk off the job, and get unemployment, or find another job. But, the idea never entered my mind. My boss had been extremely supportive throughout my employment at the agency and I could not leave him when I felt he needed me the most. What *was* really hard for me during this time was that my boss and I constantly fought about very minor things, in

the midst of this major problem the company was experiencing.

In truth, we were both stressed. The past few months had taken its toll on me mentally and physically. Due to the loss of funds, I had to give up my apartment and move back home. This was not easy, given the fact that living on my own had meant everything to me. It represented my independence, something, even to this day, I treasure. To make matters worse, the drive home was an hour, one way. This meant I could not go home if the office closed early and try to rest, and so, my days were increased by two hours each day, with the travel. By the end of my already long day, it was hard for me to wind down and relax each evening. To this very day, I have problems relaxing and falling asleep. I could only wonder about the toll it must have taken on my boss, with a whole agency and its problems on his shoulders.

Since there was nowhere for me to go in the agency, I knew it was time for me to leave and to grow. I had spent the last three years preparing to be the professional I had always dreamed of becoming one day. I knew I had to leave, but there was no way I could leave my boss or my clients when morale was at an all time low. I had to stick with him, just until things got straight, and the staff was stable once again.

I started to pray, "Lord, you know I need a new job. Lord, I want to move back out on my own, I can't continue to live like this. My body is tired and I don't know how much longer I can go on." Then, I remembered, I had several motivational tapes I had acquired from some of the many workshops I had attended over the years. I

started to listen to them over and over again, on my way to and from work. After some time had passed, I actually started to feel better, the drive was more bearable, and I started to feel more at peace. But I still had problems, I wanted to move into my own place, I wanted to get more rest and I needed more money, I *really needed* more money.

After about a month or so, I said, "God, I am going to add morning prayer to my schedule and this time I am going to have faith (even though I still didn't know what faith really was). I won't give up until something happens; even then, I am going to continue to pray in the mornings." And I started praying each morning, asking God to do something to help me and my situation.

Well, not long afterwards, things started to change. We were reimbursed for the seven months we hadn't been paid. The staff was trying to get steady again, but we had a ways to go and although I was ready to find work and grow, leaving the job was still not foreseeable. This was the difficult part. I was still having problems moving out to new living quarters because my current income would not suffice. I needed another job. By this time I had started listening to Iyanla Vanzant's motivational tape *The Value in The Valley*. This tape constantly reflected on faith, what it meant and how these times prepared us for the times ahead. Well, I listened to this tape over and over. Something had to give. I had put in job applications and sent resumes' all over, to anyplace that was hiring. Then, it finally hit me. I had not been exhibiting any faith. How could I? I didn't even know what faith was! Yes, I read the bible scriptures about *Faith being the substance of things hoped for, and the evidence of things unseen*. Well, if I

didn't see it, it was hard to have any kind of belief in it. I was really afraid of not knowing what would happen. But this time, I wanted to have faith. The only problem was, I did not know where to look. It wasn't on the other end of my phone, or in the mailbox offering me a job.

So, there I was, still miserable, looking for a job, still trying to find some peace and trying to find this thing I had just claimed as *faith*. It seemed to be getting down to the wire and I was still looking for a new job, still fighting my boss, and still traveling two extra hours a day. But, I maintained my ritual. I prayed in the morning and at night just before I went to bed. Sometimes, I found myself praying during off hours of the day. Peace started to come, but not fast enough. I was still frustrated, but I did not give up my commitment to prayer and faith.

I was talking to a friend shortly afterwards, someone I had not seen in quite some time. As she learned of my situation, she made a phone call on my behalf and took a copy of my resume' faxing it to a friend who was looking for someone to fill an administrative position at their agency. It wasn't long after that, I was called in for an interview and offered the job, on the spot. I wanted to jump, but my loyalty would not let me just leave like that. I explained it to the potential employer and he said he understood and he promised to hold the position for me. Two weeks later, I made a commitment to myself and I decided that I would leave and work part time, 9:00 a.m. to 11:45 a.m. on my current job and full time on my new one. I would go in at noon and work until 8:00 p.m. and just bypass lunch.

I had it all worked out. I went to my new office and asked "When do you want me to start?"

He responded, "You are licensed, aren't you?"

I said "No, I am undergoing supervision and I will be tested in two years."

He explained that he was sorry but, he could not give me the job and that his agency needed a board certified social worker. There was just no way I could have filled that bill, I had not been out of graduate school four good months, and there was a two-year minimum supervision period before I could even qualify for the test. I could see the hurt in his eyes. He had all but promised me the job, but the board would not allow him to hire me and there was nothing he could do. Even though I understood, my heart sank to my feet. God had answered my prayers with a big fat NO. Then I realized, that this was just a test, at least, I hoped so. Although water swelled in my eyes, I fought the tears back. I was as mad as I was hurt. And I did not know what to do. And prayer was the last thing on my mind so, I went back to my office and sat there for the remainder of the day, crushed, waiting for the time to pass.

When I got home, I told my mother about my disappointment and I said "God is only making room for something better to come along." We retired to our rooms, I know I said those words but my heart was having a hard time believing them. Before I went to bed, I said my prayers and told God I was not giving up on Him. I had to believe that I would find something soon.

The next morning, I started to question my so-called faith. I

started to talk directly to God saying, "I know you said I should have faith, and I do. What must I do to prove to you, that I believe that you can and will see me through? Lord, do you want me to walk off my job with nothing to look forward to, in order to prove to you I do believe in you, and that you can and will, see me through?" I asked that over and over, then finally, I said, "God, if you want me to walk off my job, let me know, show me a sign and I will." Well, that sign never came, but I was willing to do just as I said I would. I was sick and tired and I was tired of being tired. When I went back to my office, I started to clean my desk out and remove all of the pictures from the wall. Why, I did not know but I had to, and I knew I would be leaving someday before the year was out, even if it was the middle of July.

Well, a Sunday or two later, I was in church and my pastor asked me to teach bible school, though God knows I did not want to do that. But, I knew I had to be obedient to God's request. I told him I would. It was a fiasco. It turned out that I was not the regular teacher, I was appointed co-chairperson of the bible school. I did not have prior experience doing this and the chairperson did not, for some reason, offer any assistance, which really angered me. But, I did have a lot of support. There were many women in the church who came aboard to help me and I will always be grateful to them. But, once again, I was at odds with my boss. I had prepared to take three days off and chair the vacation bible school and let the staff manage the rest of the week without me. My new responsibilities demanded that I not take days off. This time it wasn't about me, it was about the

will of God. I was going to do what was asked of me, no matter what. So, I had planned to go into work when I left vacation bible school and just deal with the consequences when I got there. To my surprise, there were no consequences to deal with when I got there. In fact, my boss had received a fax about a job opening at an agency for a program director and he had recommended me for the position.

When I returned to work in the middle of vacation bible school, the executive director called and requested that I send my resume' via fax. Soon afterwards, the director called and set a date for an interview. The interview was about a week or so off and I was prayerful the whole time. I also expected everybody I knew to be prayerful, I requested prayer from everyone I came in contact with who knew I was looking for a job. Somewhere on one of those motivational tapes, I remembered the speaker saying "Don't try to do it alone, get yourself a prayer partner." Well, for me, one wasn't enough. Before it was over, I had a *Prayer Group*. By the time the day of the interview had arrived, I was a nervous wreck. I kept a copy of *Acts of Faith* near and constantly read and prayed. This was the most intense interview I had ever had. I was interviewed by six board members, and the executive director. I was sweating and praying all the way through. The interview was over after two of the longest hours I had ever known. I was on my way home and for the first time in a while, there was no tension within me, instead, a peace started to settle within. By the time I got home, I received the news that I was the new program director, with a nine thousand-dollar increase in pay. My response was "Thank you, Jesus!!!"

I thought about what Iyanla Vanzant said about faith and it really did ring true: This is her definition of faith.

When you come to the end of all of the light you know and you are about to step off into the darkness, Faith is knowing one of two things will happen: there be something solid in the darkness for you to stand on, or you will be taught to fly.

That night, I was finally learning how to fly.

Yolanda E. Scott, MSW
New Orleans, LA

A Blessing In Disguise

It was a day of mixed emotions as I left Georgia to embark on my new job in New Jersey. My sister had a going-away dinner to give me a great send off. My nieces did not fully understand what was happening, but my other family members did. I knew this job would be the start of another chapter in my life. I was leaving my home, my friends, and family to pursue this new career.

I never will forget as I pulled out of the driveway, my family waving until I was no longer in view. Tears engulfed my eyes, as I was leaving everything familiar I knew. Was I making the right choice, I started to question myself? I felt like turning around and going back to my sister's house and telling my new boss, I would not be coming. Quickly, something inside said "That, is not the thing to do. You are an overcomer, you can handle this move." So, I drove my rent-a-car to Hartsfield International Airport and got on the plane, ready to embark on my new adventure.

I cried silently on the plane, as the void I felt inside ached my soul. I knew this career move would be a life changing experience for

me. My strength and inner spirit would have to sustain me.

I arrived in New Jersey and drove to the hotel for my one week stay, that turned into an assignment lasting three months. I moved from hotel to hotel, as I traveled in my new job. This only added to my query of wondering had I made the right choice. Doubt slowly began to enter my mind and caused additional stress in my life. Stress, at this time, I did not need.

Finally, three months later, I moved into my new home. It was a day of rejoicing. Now, I felt I could get settled and start meeting people and things would get better. To my chagrin, this did not happen because of my busy traveling schedule. After all this time, I still knew almost no one. Yes, I met some of the people at work, but no true bonds had been established. I was still very alone. I dreaded the start of the weekend because, out there in that big, empty house, there was only me. I looked forward to Monday coming so I could be around people. "What a life I had chosen!" I thought to myself. This was not at all like I had pictured it to be.

I would look in the mirror and say, "What have I done to deserve this loneliness?" I cried most of the weekends away, anxiously awaiting my return to work on Monday. I spent evenings and weekends by myself, it was a difficult time in my life. I finally started to meet people as my traveling schedule started to decline, but I was still spending most of the time by myself. One day, it dawned on me this was part of the growth process. I had to get in touch with myself and learn to depend on Nancy. I had to go back to my spiritual foundation. God had not left me, I had left Him, as I wallowed in my

pity. I was trying to handle this move on my own and I simply realized that I needed God's guidance to help me cope. I started to release the anger, hurt, and resentment I was feeling, replacing those feelings with love, as I started seeking the lesson God wanted me to learn in this situation.

Needless to say, I started meeting more people and my life started to change. You see, I had been carrying a lot of negative baggage and now I had replaced that baggage with positive energy and love. I truly began to love myself and trust myself and most importantly trust God. You see, God never leaves us. He is waiting for us to be obedient and let Him direct our path. This seemingly dismal, challenging situation had become a blessing in disguise.

I realized that whom God calls, he equips. Everything I needed to handle the move, I had within. God had given me the tools all along. I simply had to open up my mind and heart and watch the miracles unfold. That move was where my speaking career began and I feel blessed today, to be doing what I love, *speaking for a living.* You see, God was the potter and He was molding and empowering me to develop my gift of speaking. So, be encouraged and know that many of our blessings in life come in disguise. Be willing to step out of your comfort zone and watch the boundaries disappear. Always do your best and leave the rest up to God!!

Nancy J. Lewis, MS, PHR
Fayetteville, GA

Shedding My Earth Suit

*H*ow do I express with the right words and emphasis, the fact that as you live and work in our society, things change? At some point, you will experience challenging periods that will have numerous beginnings and endings. Your days begin and end, careers, relationships, and friendships all have a beginning and ending. I can firmly say, "There are no magical formulas for a prosperous, productive and glorious life." Every activity requires super human inner strength and a strong desire for discipline and balance. Just as God's creatures must shed their shells, skins, and layers to transform their existence, we too, must learn to shed our earth suits and find our inner spirits before we can become our real true spirits.

As I approach major milestones in my working career of 37 years in the workforce, I believe that it is just as important to celebrate the ending of jobs, as it is to rejoice at the beginning. Each event brings with it a transitional period of pain, growth and courage to continue onward and upward.

I was born in Aberdeen, Mississippi where there were no wealthy warriors in my background that I could identify with, who could inspire me to acquire a successful, prosperous career. All of the women in my family line have been hard working, cooks, maids, housekeepers, nurses and domestic workers. Their careers started at

sun up and ended at sun down. The most valuable information they imparted to me was to always work and make money to survive. I started working at age 13, to help my Mother support our family. Now, after working more than 25 different types of jobs I am convinced that every transition happens for some unknown reason, and that you may only discover that reason after having been loyal to your responsibility at that time.

It is amazing how much of what we do for a living impacts who we are. Sometimes our job titles and positions are attached to our economic status, living conditions, social status, and ultimately, our self-esteem.

It is not uncommon to attend activities and events and get introduced by your name and job title, such as, "This is Miss B. She is the Director for Bell Company." These are all great beginnings. However, endings happen when you experience the transition of job loss, no money, lost wages, divorce, death and other uncertainties and fears.

A serious transition began for me when I found myself unemployed for one year and eleven months. My life went through a series of changes that rearranged my attitude about work, careers, relationships, and what God's plan was for my life. There were two major activities that helped me to keep my sanity. My routine of documenting daily in my diary my feelings of stress, emotional pain and the times of extreme joy and my daily meditation periods in my prayer closet.

In December 1993, I was laid off from my job on a Thursday,

diagnosed with a skin disorder on Friday, and experienced the death of a close friend by the following Monday. As a single parent, each of these activities was an ending to some of my life activities and a beginning to others. It was a hurting experience to lose my job, right before Christmas. But, to also deal with a major health problem at the same time was very devastating. Little did I know that my life was going to change again rapidly.

I was accustomed to struggling to remain in college and pinching pennies or as my son says, "living on the edge of life." I was determined to finish the graduate program I was in, because after all, it had taken me 17 years to complete my undergraduate studies and I knew that another degree would help change our way of living and boost my career. But, what I didn't know was that God had a bigger plan. My faith could sustain the job loss but my looks and my health meant more to me than anything, because I always wanted to be a professional trainer.

For days, I was unable to function or make any sense out of what was happening to me. I began to follow the normal channels for a job search, but my heart just was not in the process. I would take my diary with me everywhere I went, so that at any spare moment, I could write my feelings down. Its important that we express our feelings and opinions because there were some things that I was feeling, that I could not say to my friends. After the fifth month of unemployment, they really didn't even bother to ask about my job search. I learned to manage with only ten dollars a week budgeted for food and gas. As I looked in the mirror, all I could see

was the damage to my earth suit, which by now was covered with scars and marks over seventy percent of my body. The only areas that were spared was my face and my legs. I could only cry when I had to take my clothes off.

When out in public, my appearance was great and my attitude was always positive. But, when alone, I cried and ached to feel good about my life and the transition I was going through. This must have been some cruel joke that was meant for someone else. Surely not me, when God knew how important my looks were to my career. How could I survive when I could not even stand to look at myself?

Daily, I would find time to meditate on God's word in my closet and hide my fears and to find out what was the plan. This was my only comfort zone. If I walked through the house, all I could see were bills, calls from bill collectors, and mirrors. I began to change my wardrobe to mostly black and dark colors. That is how I felt inside my heart, as it throbbed with pain, as my skin (earth suit) was continuing to change colors. I began to seek help from doctors, advice from holistic personnel, anyone who could render support to my condition and provide guidance. When I would show my under skin to my friends, I could tell by the looks on their faces that my situation was bad. As attractive a woman as I used to be, that hurt even more. So, I stopped seeking help from friends and even family members.

I was so excited the day I got my first contract job as a trainer. When I was told that I would be a trainer in front of a large audience, you can imagine how disappointed I was, that God would have given me a job like that when I was so uncomfortable with my appearance.

During this transition period, I also began to make sporadic decisions about my life and what I should do. I remember that I could never sleep for very long. I would wake up at 4:00am every morning and go to my closet for guidance and inner strength. I prayed and asked for directions, and was led to move after graduation. It was revealed that I should move near my home town and family. I felt that if I could only go home, things would get better. Two days after graduation, I packed everything I had and moved from my home of 17 years to seek bonding and peace with my family. This move was between me and God. I needed a change. I was running to a different life style, so I thought. Things were fine, for a while, because I was in a different city and out of my comfort zone. However, the transition wasn't over. I literally walked and cried for two months, trying to discover God's plan for my life. What is my purpose? Where am I going? I had nothing left, our money was low, all my furniture and material things were in a box. My skin was more irritated from the stress. Of course, I found a closet to pour my heart out. My diary pages were filled each day. All I could say was, "God, what is the plan?"

As soon as I got still and refused to cry anymore, or see myself in a negative light, I heard a voice say, GO HOME. I didn't understand, I didn't have a home, but I knew the voice meant back to Atlanta. Oh God, how could I go back, I would look so stupid. My furniture is gone, my job is gone, my looks were gone, my money was gone, all I had were three degrees, a son, and my car. I ran to the closet and

prayed. "God, if this is to happen, I will get out of the way and let you lead me. Only you can work this out."

Within five days, super natural miracles began to appear in my personality and my attitude. I was told by the spirit to sell the rest of my furniture and only take what I could in my car. Oh, I felt so silly. Trying to return with nothing! But, in late August, 1995, during my evening meditation with God, I asked for a new me, with a firmly grounded spirit, stronger and tougher than before to see me through this transition to victory.

As I made preparations to make my journey back home to Atlanta, I did not come back the same person. I felt a spiritual shedding of my old skin to reveal a new and improved me. I was not the same person that I was in 1993. The fear of job loss has motivated me to train others to embrace change and understand that a job might not be what God wants for you right away.

Unemployment can be a time for healing, sharing, and discovering new meanings to life. We all have different types of earth suits that we wear every day. I needed to shed my need to control, and dominate every thing in my life.

What I found is a humble side of myself that needed a daily relationship with God. My inner spirit needed attention. I believe that attention came to me through my skin. My healing is coming and I thank God every day. I still don't know every aspect of the plan for my life. But it's OK, God knows. I am at peace with my life.

I am working in the career I always wanted as a professional trainer, my son is healthy, and I have a wonderful new home. God has opened new doors of opportunity for me. I just trusted that there would be a beginning and ending. Through this transition I was able to shed my old earth suit and find a new spirit full of light and energy, that embraces changes as a rebirth to life.

Tom Ella McBeth
Riverdale, GA

From Rags to Riches

$\mathcal{I}$t happened like Cinderella. Along came this handsome man riding up in a shiny new convertible. He swept me off my feet. I was presented with gifts of fine cars, boats, clothes for every occasion, and very expensive jewelry. I lived in a house that sat on a hill, overlooking a lake and the whole community. We traveled several times a year and had involved the children in things where they were the only children of color. I didn't work outside the home and was involved in many community affairs. You name it, I had it. Anything I thought my little heart wanted, I got. But, then one day .... it was gone! Everything material we had owned was snatched away.

Prince charming lost his job. Our world came crashing in all around us. We didn't know which way to turn. No job matched the salary, prestige, or benefits that my husband was accustomed to. Slowly, we watched our world fall apart, right before our eyes. We lost it all, everything. My husband turned to drinking, drugs, and the streets. I didn't know what to do. I was so caught up in all the material things I had, I forgot to put Christ first in our lives.

I started questioning God. Why me? What have I done to deserve this? Christ had always been a part of my life, but we were

too busy enjoying the material things to fully give Christ praise and recognition. I realized that Christ gives to us, but also takes away from us. I kept telling my husband, we have our health, strength, friends, and family. Those are things money cannot buy. I had to get strong in the word and strengthen my faith, so I could keep my family together.

My husband was so distraught, that he wouldn't hold a job for any length of time. With three children, no steady income, and good health, I knew I had to find work. I hadn't worked in over eight years. My skills were terrible. I went on the first interview, and was told I had the job. Can you imagine how I felt! It wasn't the best paying job, but it was steady income and provided us with good health benefits. God is good, all the time, and all the time God is good.

I started going to church on a regular basis. The more problems that tumbled around me, the stronger I found my faith getting. There is so much more I can add to this story, it could go on for days. God had to humble my spirit. He dealt with me in a way that even to this day, I still tell people, "Put God first and all other things will be added unto you." God had to show me it is not material wealth that makes us happy, but serving Him.

I thank God for everything he has blessed me with. I know He will supply my needs, not everything I think I want, but my needs! What a wonderful feeling that is. I have peace of mind, good health and strength, family, friends, and most of all, God in my life. One of my favorite scriptures is found in Phillipians 4:11 *(Not that I speak in*

respect of want: for I have learned, in whatsoever state I am, therewith to be content). Thank you, God for all that you have blessed me with. Thank you, thank you, thank you!

You can now understand why I gave this short story the title "Rags to Riches." Even though I lost all the material things I owned in the world, they were no more than rags.

I was blessed with riches from God above that this world cannot provide for me. We don't understand why things happen to us, but God has a lesson for every trial He puts us through. I learned from this lesson to develop a more humble and giving spirit.

Patricia Munford
College Park, GA

Why Me? - One Of Life's Important Lessons

*G*rowing up in a middle class family until I was 14, allowed me to be fairly sheltered from many things that most of my friends had already experienced, most particularly - drugs! I married my husband at 26 and he was 28. We had dated for a year and some months, so we were fairly sure that we were made for one another. He was kind, generous, loving, affectionate, intelligent.....everything a woman could want in a man. Oh yes, one thing I left out - he was a drug addict. And that's where my roller coaster ride to reality began! He was addicted to crack cocaine and I, (Miss sheltered and naive) didn't have a clue! At first, I thought it was another woman, but I soon found - crack, is like *another woman,* only I couldn't compete with her. She plays dirty, she seduces, she occupies his mind constantly and she just wouldn't let go, no matter what I did! I told my husband that we could work it out together, you know, love our way through it — Yeah, Right!

I thought being the perfect wife would give him a reason to stop. I thought keeping the house clean would keep him home

instead of the crack house. I thought being the ideal mother would make him at least think twice about it. I ran the gamut - I was loving and attentive, I was mean and hateful, I was angry and resentful, I was distant and brooding — Nothing worked! Through all this, I was praying to God but not giving it to Him, completely. I'd pray and then try to fix it myself. One day, I cried to God, "Why me, God. Why am I going through this?" I had been diagnosed with Lupus two years before, and of course the illness had taken its toll on me, and the stress of my marriage just added fuel to an already raging fire.

One day, as I was driving around looking for my husband, who had not been home in three days, God began to talk to me. He answered my question "Why Me?" with a question, "Why not You?" He said, "You will be a living testimony of how pain can be turned to joy and how weakness will make you a tower of strength. You will testify to others and bring them to Me for Power, Love, Patience, and Endurance to run the race that I have set before you." From that moment, I knew that everything in life happens for a divine reason and if you don't learn from it, you're destined to repeat it.

And so the days and nights of tears, heartbreak, lies, deceptions, being penniless, homeless, and hopeless continued. So did the months of rehabilitation, jail, no diapers or milk, abandonment, and being what is called, co-dependent and an enabler, to a liar, and a cheat. The constant circus of robbing Peter to pay Paul, the arguments and fights, the lost of friends and relationships, the lost jobs and productive time turned into three years. At the expense of my self-esteem, my confidence, my trust and love, I finally packed up

my boys and I left. I could take no more....I was on the edge (very close to falling off). I felt like a failure as a mother, a wife and a woman. I couldn't sleep, eat or talk. I couldn't express my thoughts or feelings to anyone. I went to counseling and for the first few weeks, I cried the entire time. I couldn't talk. I just poured out all of those years of hurt, loneliness, disappointment and anger. I had to release everything. Finally, when I could talk, I joined a support group for co-dependents. There were men and women in the group. It's funny when you here the testimonies of one, you've pretty much heard all of them. We all had the same stories of manipulation, lying, cheating and to some degree, a similar story as to how we came to the group.

After I began to see myself again... Me, the confident woman that I was before I met him, the lively, young woman, who was focused on her career and her life's goals, I began to grow again emotionally and spiritually. My confidence grew to levels to exceed all my dreams. You know what God showed me? I learned that I had to love myself enough to say "Enough is Enough!" I learned that I couldn't "fix" my husband. I learned that I could not save my husband, only God could. I learned that drug addiction is an illness, but also it's a matter of will. I learned that I have a greater capacity to love anyone, unconditionally. But ultimately, I learned to love myself and God without measure. Now, I can love others in a healthy, loving and mature manner.

Twanda Black
College Park, GA

Lessons From a Three Year Old

*B*everly! No word ever written could do her justice. This tiny brown haired blue eyed, two year old child could melt ones heart in a minute. She had a beautiful smile. It was the type of smile that could make all of your worries disappear. Her eyes were the windows to her hardships and experience of her short life that some people could only have nightmares about.

God blessed our family with Beverly when she was placed in our home as a foster child. She was truly an angel. She was like a beautiful flower blossoming and growing every day. When she first came to our home, she would stare in quiet confusion with her thumb as her only comfort. Time went by and Beverly blossomed into a talkative young girl. She had such a beautiful free spirit and seemed to adjust to the love our family gave her. In the year and a half she lived with us, we came to love her and spent many a night praying that she would not have to return to her family.

God finally answered our prayers, but not in the way we expected. It was on a beautiful sunny day in August that Beverly fell

into our pool unnoticed and drowned. She had graced this earth for three short years and lived among our family for only a year and a half. Her life was short but oh, what an impact she had on my life. My grief was inconsolable for months. Oh, how I missed her. Looking back, I realize that God put this angel in our home to teach me four lessons that I now pass on to others in my trainings and keynotes.

The first lesson is about love. Beverly would always run to her mother and father with outstretched arms and leap into their laps. I would stand there in amazement, every time I witnessed this scene. Oh, how she loved her parents. It was during these visits that I realized that the heart of a child loves, unconditionally. We can spank them, send them to their rooms or treat them with a lack of respect, and they always come back with outstretched arms, filled with love. I was once three. I used to love, unconditionally. What happened between three and thirty three? Every time I see Beverly's picture, I am reminded to forgive, not judge and love people, unconditionally, just as God forgives me and loves me, unconditionally. Whom do you need to love, unconditionally?

The second lesson is about wisdom. Beverly was just getting to that age where she was asking questions "Why, Mommy? How does this work, Mommy? What does this do, Mommy?" It seemed like the questions would never stop. In quiet reflection, I now realize that God gave Beverly the ability to ask questions so that she could seek wisdom. It is only in the asking of questions that we truly learn the answers to survive in our daily lives. I once was three. I used to ask questions. Somewhere along the way, someone told me to put

my hand down and not ask so many questions. I did. I stopped seeking wisdom. God wants me to ask questions. He wants me to learn. He wants me to seek his wisdom and teach it to others. I have begun to ask questions again. Are you asking questions and seeking his knowledge?

The third lesson is about joy. As the months passed and Beverly became secure with our family, her joy and laughter filled our home. Beverly would always wake up my daughter Alicia with the words "Wake up, Alicia! It's time to play." Oh, the joy and laughter Beverly had. I was once, three. I used to have joy and laughter. Where did it go? As adults we get so caught up in the seriousness of life and forget to laugh. I have begun to laugh again. I have begun to laugh and be joyous, just as God wants me to be. I know he wants that for us. The word joy is mentioned eighteen times just in one book of of the Bible. He wants us to be joyous and free with the truth of His word. Are you joyous and free?

The final lesson I learned from Beverly is that she did not go to school to learn any of the above mentioned qualities. I realized that Beverly did not go to school to learn how to love. It is natural. She did not go to school to learn how to ask questions. It is natural. She did not go to school to learn how to laugh. It is natural. And never did I see Beverly with a to do list or worry about life. That is something she did not get to experience because she was not here on earth long enough to have life's experiences cover up her ability to love, ask questions, and be joyous and free. The good news is that we all can make a conscious choice to overcome the fears that prevent us

from living our lives as Beverly did in her three short years here on earth.

Two years have passed since Beverly was called to a place where she has more than her thumb to comfort her. She is still missed deeply. I am so grateful for the lessons she taught, not only me, but also to those to whom I pass the message on to. This story is in memory of this angel sent to me from above.

Abby Shields, MEd
Mandeville, LA

Simple Things Remind Me

*S*he had come to realize that one of the disadvantages of traveling anywhere the first time was that you were always subject to error when plotting the time it takes to get to the airport. So once again, she'd almost missed the plane.

It had been her first time traveling to Minnesota and though she had thoroughly enjoyed the trip, she was real happy to be going home. Now she could catch her breath and begin once again, the metamorphosis from high powered business woman, to Nia's mother, Alex's wife, Madear's daughter, Pop's "sweetie pie," J'heron's best friend and the list goes on. So much so, that she almost became breathless at the thought of everything that waited for her at home.

Lately, things at the office had been chaotic. A layoff was rumored and the worst in human nature was surfacing. And though she understood what was happening and why, she still felt the effects. The work environment, her performance and her confidence were suffering.

Here she was, on her way home and maybe now wasn't the time to think about distress on the job. Maybe, she should just feel her way through the transition. Involved in this little debate with herself,

she was suddenly made aware of the here and now by a soothing voice that greeted them with, "Ladies and gentlemen, I am John Burke, your pilot for this evening on your nonstop flight to Atlanta." She smiled to herself as she imagined him to be a D.J. The pilot continued with, "We will be flying at an altitude of 22,000 feet. Weather reports indicate that we may pass through some mild turbulence and we are asking you to keep your seat belts on until the seat belt indicator light goes out."

She'd heard so many of these pilot greetings that she could almost do them herself. Anyhow, it seemed safe to tune him out, so she shifted her attentions and went back to trying to relax not really noticing or hearing anything else.

After a short nap, she became a little restless and decided to take out her book. She was once again reading *Their Eyes Were Watching God.* She read it every once and awhile when she needed to be optimistic or wanted to reach the vulnerable part of herself that sometimes was buried so deep that it needed help finding its way out. And, most of all, she read the book because it helped to remind her that there is a Master Plan and that God is indeed the architect.

So, she read on. Janie, the central character meets this fellow called Teacake, a charming, but suspect man. Anyone reading the book for the first time might be concerned for Janie. You know those men. They'll mess up your life and then, poof, they're gone. All of sudden, with a smirk she caught herself. Oops, she was getting all riled up. What in the world did she have to be bitter about? Her mother and father were still married and enjoying forty years of

marriage. And her husband Alex was a real gem. He supported her, was hard working himself, was very conscientious about working on his woman "crap."

She even looked forward to their hot discussions on "What do you women want anyway, blood?" He was a great father and he loved the very ground she walked on. And with a child from a previous relationship things were complicated sometimes. She admired how he maintained a good relationship with his son and with his son's mother and how he'd orchestrated a good relationship between Alex Jr. and her.

Well, maybe it was just one of those times that she felt bitter about all the friends she'd comforted. Or maybe she was just plain scared that her success at beating the odds might be over one day. After all, it seems virtually impossible to be both a successful, black woman, professionally, who is also successful in a black/female relationship.

Well...now she'd done it. She'd worked herself up into a real tizzy again. She was now too anxious to read, and besides, Janie would keep. So, she decided to get a glass of wine lay back and listen to some of her oldie but goodie tapes. She always carried them with her too, because they were therapeutic. They had a way of reminding her of the time when she really believed that she was invincible.

Smiling she remembered, she was really full of the herself in those days. Now, every once and a while she lost that confidence and she needed reminding. And, more than anything, music helped her to center and find herself. When those old songs played, she was

almost able to smell the smells, and hear the voices that shared the song with her in the past. And so, she listened to Marvin Gaye and Tammi Terrell, Stevie Wonder, Curtis Mayfield, Donny Hathaway, yes, and Ashford and Simpson.

She must have dozed off to sleep too because it was maybe thirty minutes later and she felt much better, calmer and more relaxed. She didn't know exactly what was different; she just knew that she felt better.

So, she took *Their Eyes Where Watching God* out again to continue her visit with Janie. The stewardess was picking up the trays from a meal. So, she must have slept for over thirty minutes. However long it was, she felt much better now. Maybe the anxiety was just her never really becoming quite comfortable with this flying thing. After all, you don't really feel the speed, and the sky and the clouds can be so very seductive, almost magical. The whole process defies logic. Sometimes, it looked like you could walk out the door and just walk on the clouds. Walk on clouds?

Right, like Warren Beatty in *Heaven Can Wait*, huh? She smiled, thinking to herself , "Come on, now, she was Danita Johnson-Mulden. How much time would she give to such craziness?"

For some reason, often recently, she wound up wondering about and sometimes even mediating on such things. Flowers, rain, sunsets, shells, clouds, the moon, stars...

She couldn't put her finger on it, but for some reason, these things captured her attention and her imaginings. She seemed moved sometimes by the fact that they even existed. Her feelings seemed to

be so accessible with a sort of vulnerable, child-like innocence.

Smiling, she thought maybe this was what experience and maturity felt like, having the common sense to grasp simple pleasure wherever and whenever you could find it.

Caught up in this dialogue with herself, she didn't even notice the gradual dimming of the daylight.

Her attention, however, was gradually nudged by this warm red glow that seemed to appear out of nowhere. Slightly alarmed in her effort to determine where it came from, she looked around herself and sniffed the air to make sure it was not fire, smoke or some reflecting alarm. Still unconvinced of safety, she turned away from the window on alert ready to move quickly with the least provocation. Finally, convinced of her safety, she settled back into her seat and once again focused her attention outside the window of the plane.

The dusky sky seemed to give way to a gradual coloring which was suddenly halted. All of a sudden she gasped, her breath was taken away by the amazing sight of the most beautiful nature expression she'd ever seen; a sunset from the sky.

The combination of the clouds had hid the sight for a while. The blues, projecting reds, and oranges, purples and pinks seemed to draw her into the power of the vivid colors. She stared, not even blinking, for fear of missing even one second. Her mind raced while she prayed for total recall or photographic memory, and in the prayer recognized the folly of the wish. Then, in resignation and frustration she just cried. The tears slid silently down her cheeks almost without

her knowing it, tears for the staggering beauty and the tender power of this sunset.

She cried because she'd never be able to share this with Alex, J'heron or her children. In fact, they'd probably think her weird for thinking it was so special. Well, J'heron wouldn't think so. But she continued to cry, because she knew that her memory of this could never quite equal the experience itself.

Then, smiling to herself, she thought maybe this was the kind of experience that helped to give her grandmother that odd, smart-alex, just-wait-and-you'll-see look. All she knew was that next to sex and seeing her baby for the first time, she had never felt anything so powerful before. Smiling to herself she then found herself humming a song she remembered from when she was a little girl. It was a song her grandfather used to sing her sometime. "Red sails in the sunset, way out on the sea. Oh, carry my loved one home safely to me." She felt good humming it to herself.

And without even realizing it, she let go of trying to do more than enjoy herself and moved easily into looking forward to getting home, home to Alex, to Nia, Madear, J'heron, and everyone and everything else that waited for her there. And, she thanked God, for all the things that helped to make her life so great. She was especially thankful for, simple everyday things like this sunset that helped to remind her sometimes, just how wonderfully blessed her life really was.

Akua Wambui (a.k.a Carol Bebelle)
New Orleans, LA

Life is a Dance!

"Gail" her name tag read. White hair, sixty-something. As the music swelled, Gail made her way across the dance floor, moving with the melody, lost in the magic of the moment. Alone. Except for an inflated heart-shaped balloon she was clutching by a streamer, part of the party decorations.

As I watched, intrigued, she brushed by my table at the edge of the dance floor, and I couldn't resist the urge to say something.

"Glad to see you dancing," I said smiling.

"I love to dance," she beamed. "My husband's feet hurt, so I decided to dance anyway . . . even if I have to dance alone."

What a testimony! Gail knows how to create her own happiness without depending on someone else to dance to her tune.

Judy Moon Denson
Hattiesburg, MS

"To See The World As It Is, And Not As I See IT"

$\mathcal{A}$ special thanks to every contributor who submitted a story for our book, *Sisters Together: Lessons Learned That Have Anchored Our Souls*. This was an exciting project and like most things I venture into, my level of enthusiasm overwhelmed even myself. I immediately prepared a timeline schedule for both Nancy and myself as we assigned specific tasks for each other. We are very focused partners with a similar determination for getting a job done.

I started telling ladies that my letter was coming in the mail. On the surface, they appeared happy and excited about participating in the project. When I say I will do something, consider it done. My letters were mailed and many of the ladies responding said, "I can't wait until I get your letter, to start writing as soon as possible." Now, I'm calling Nancy practically every night. "Nancy, this project is going to be wonderful. A real shot in the arm." And, she's feeling just as exhilarated.

Of course, three weeks later, judgment sets in. There were no responses from the contributors. Those ordinary human tendencies

and negative thoughts were settling in and I knew better. But I admit, I did entertain some uneasy feelings. If someone had asked me to do something, one way or another, they would get feedback from me. I would at least respond with a 'yes' or 'no' commitment. The requester would know my position immediately, as to if I could contribute a story or my schedule was too hectic.

The letters went out early in September, 1997. Immediately, a National Speakers Association member called to say she was overcommitted. "Debra, Good Luck on your project. Unfortunately, I'm also writing my second book so I cannot contribute time to your project." I respected that feedback because this is how I operate. One month prior to the deadline I suggested to Nancy that we should conduct follow-up calls. Nancy said people will probably wait until the last minute. We're all so busy. Although I already knew the kind of women in our network are busy women, they 'really have it going on.' My spirit was feeling a little weak. In my heart, I knew the women I know will deliver because they are powerful and dynamic women. So, I decided to back off.

I realized that I was so caught up with my own excitement that I hadn't prayed for this blessing. God created this incredible opportunity for Nancy and Debra to ask for all of these dynamic women's tremendous support, love and to share stories from their hearts. We asked for those stories we all often talk about over the phone, in letters to each other, over lunch breaks, and at dinner meetings. After praying for this blessing, a calmness and a peace came over me. A few days later, I began making phone calls. The women

in my network started asking, "Debra, what are you writing about?" They were relaxed and eager to contribute now, following my call. These women were honored by my request and even shared, "You want *me* to write something?" They couldn't even conceive authoring a story or a book. I had affirmed this book project and it became just another goal to achieve. Other friends said "Would you mind sharing your story to help 'Anchor my Soul' in the right direction." So, I faxed or e-mailed my story to them. It was just phenomenal, what was taking place in my connection with all of these powerful contributors.

A remarkable awareness occurred, I stopped being judgmental. I released those wasted and worrisome thoughts that were messing with my head, about folks not wanting to support my book project. I didn't let those thoughts rob me of the positive energy this book project needed to succeed. After all, the deadline was November 1, 1997. I didn't panic. I put my energies into writing my own story. From that moment on, I let go of any fears and insecurities. I let go and let God.

Two weeks before the deadline, everyday there were stories flowing in. The book project was truly a growth period for me, as well. I was able to shift my fears and cope with reality. I was now able to experience my gratitude and appreciation for those contributors who really cared enough to take time out of their busy schedules to show Nancy and Debra their love. They were reminding me that I, too, contribute and bring something to our relationship. What was so phenomenal, both Mary Kay Kurzweg and Barbara

Cypher submitted three stories. Both Mary Kay and Barbara said "Debra, we trust you will select the appropriate story." A marvelous revelation happened as each contributor was sending their feedback to me. Their expressions came by phone, e-mail, fax, and postcards. Here's a few of their love notes: "Debra, just wanted to let you know simply how much I appreciate your many gifts of sharing and caring to include me on this book project." "Debra, thanks kindly for asking me to contribute a story." "Debra, just when I think you have done it all, here you go and take it to another level." "Debra, thank you for giving me this opportunity to tell my story." "Debra, thank you for including me in your dream project." "Debra, thank you for considering me in this project." "Debra, I'm shocked that you believe I have something to share and contribute." "Debra, you sure know how to elevate others and take your friends and business associates for a joyful ride on your continuous journey." "Debra, you know how to touch and reach people's hearts in a positive way."

Every day my focus challenges me to expand more as a human being. Their stories moved me personally. In addition, their special notes weaved a common thread. There was a rebirth and renewing energy level igniting from my own soul as their stories moved me personally. Every woman touched my life and there was value added for them, as well. God revealed names of friends I had omitted who contributed in other ways. Renette Dejoie Hall, publisher and editor, agreed to give me a write up when we release the book. Talk about a phenomenal woman! She's all that, and more. She said "Debra, if you are involved in this project "Its ALL GOOD" please count me in. In

fact, I will go a step further. Let me feature this book release in the March 1998 Louisiana Weekly Publishing Company issue." So, now I am focused again, and feeling wonderful, uplifted and upbeat as usual. I looked around my office and staring at me was my favorite line *"Persistence Beats Resistance Every Time."* This tagline was created by Tina Thomas, a professional speaker and author. She said, "Debra, when I think of you and when I'm around you, these are the words that describe your excitement, enthusiasm for life and your determination to be a winner."

This experience taught me well, that there are a lot of people who look at me and say, "Oh, I can do what she's doing." That's the kind of influence I want to have on people. I talk about this in my programs. In life its so easy to say "I can" do what someone else is doing. But, they rarely do it. The formula for my success is deeply rooted in sticking to my action plan. I never allow myself to say I'm not good enough. I will say, "Implement now and perfect later." That is a saying made famous by Larry Winget. I am more a "I Will" believer versus a "I Can" person. I know inside me I have already determined my victory and it's "All Good." I have embraced God, as my source of energy to believe in my capacity, abilities, talents, and skills. From this belief, I have a self-acceptance that anchors my soul. Now, my energies are channeled in thinking truly about my blessings because this was a blessing from God, to have planted this seed for Nancy and Debra.

The origin of *Sisters Together* is more clearly defined for me now. When I think about Nancy and Debra coming together, we were struggling entrepreneurs. When I think about *Sisters Together* it is

Nancy and Debra's victory story. Two brilliant entrepreneurs coming together as partners. We operate and own separate businesses. But Together, we are stronger. On occasion we collaborate and take on joint ventures. Our separate businesses have grown because of our sisterly relations. We often refer each other for business with potential clients as trainers, consultants, and professional speakers. We both conduct leadership, team building, and interpersonal skills training. What's different is our uniqueness and specialized areas that Nancy conducts training in customer service and Debra conducts training in diversity in the workplace. We bounce ideas off each other and brainstorm on a regular basis. *Sisters Together* (partnering) has been a confidence building process. The *Sisters Together* concept has added new meaning to the word partnership. Love for our professional business, love for our work, and love for each other allows us grow with abundance, happiness, and prosperity. Nancy was the glue for me and the contributors' stories helped anchor my soul to keep on soaring. This relationship has kept me grounded and lastly, it keeps me centered on the Almighty GOD. Lesson Learned: I am a world overcomer and through daily prayer, I remind myself that I have the power "To see the world as it is, and not as I see it." I deal with my doubts, obstacles, and fears, releasing them to the Almighty GOD, and with calmness, reassurance, and courage, they will all end up GOOD.

Debra Washington Gould, MS
New Orleans, LA

I Am Too Blessed To Be Stressed

*W*hat do I mean? Well, when a person gets to this emotional level some trying experience has definitely occurred to rock your world. If you believe that you are a world overcomer, nothing and nobody can block your blessings. It wasn't easy getting to this point in my life. In fact, I probably spent 20 years just trying to figure this process out. I finally learned through painful lessons, how to eliminate distress and negativity in my life.   Sometimes, those negative experiences caused me to shut down, as negativity consumed my thoughts. I had to learn to let go, because it was affecting my creativity. After years of wasted time, I learned that when you trust in God, and His unstoppable faith, you come to realize your own inner strength.

Most of my bad encounters were experienced in the workplace, and from professional people. Working in an atmosphere of petty envy, professional jealousy, and pessimistic people can drag you down. These factors made going through the daily routines in a work environment unpleasant and marginally productive. In my department, I worked mostly around white men who were threatened by a strong female who was African American. We all know that a positive person cannot change a negative person. There

were issues there, that had nothing to do with your ability to get the job done. Mostly, those issues were facing each day and working around insecure employees. They were threatened by your credentials, skills, and credibility. I often asked the question, "Why are people so mean? Why are people such nasty human beings?" I sat down with my mentor, James Wallace one day who said, "They are afraid of you, afraid that you are better than them." The best thing one can do is to stay clear of pessimistic people and troublemakers. While there is no place to escape, you just do not frequent the circles they would travel. Yes, it was very hard to remain focused on your purpose for being there. Through prayer and self-control, one must focus on their talents, skills, and purpose to realize you can persist, and that you must not quit. I had focus and channeled my energy into upgrading my professional skills and taking advantage of company training courses to enhance my professional skills. I'm so glad I did exactly that.

As it turned out, those troublemakers are no longer employed at the same company. Their skills became obsolete which made my skills more marketable. They were too busy trying to keep a good woman down, who was also a qualified African-American who performed her duties well. They didn't understand the power of faith. Little did those men know I was developing my own inner strength to cope with the difficulties in the work environment. I set some rules for my internal processing and mental well-being. Just simple statements to keep me anchored and focused on work related tasks. If I heard negative talk or confrontations, I would immediately say,

Rule #1: Don't sweat the small stuff. Rule #2: When the situation occurring now is managed well, it's all small stuff. Let it go. What I have experienced in these situations was, their silly games were just small stuff. We have all worked around negative people, office politics, and hostile work environments. They cannot be avoided. We have all encountered those individuals who can find bad news and spread it around the office until everybody is talking and reacting to the bad news, instead of what is productive and what is the truth.

I decided that it is up to me and it was my responsibility to set the tone of each day. No matter how troubled I was feeling about this bad working experience, it was up to me to be the captain of my ship and navigate my ship to shore. I was responsible for creating the possibilities in turning things around when there were bad times. I discovered something interesting. First, I began writing a diary and recalling my feelings, thoughts and ideas. Second, I began to internalize the positive experiences in my life. Third, I began to take action and realized I was responsible for the outcome and results in my life. Fourth, I began reading positive and motivational books. Fifth, I sought counseling from a support group. Sixth, I began to write down my goals and success plan for living. Lastly, I discovered it works because I have chosen happiness as a purpose for living.

A remarkable thing happened, I started each day feeling energized. Each night I would fall down on my knees and give thanks to my Heavenly Father. Just to say thank you. I didn't have to say what it was because God already knows it, before I think it or speak it. Each morning when I woke up I would say "Thank you for a new

day, Almighty God." Every morning I have made a pledge to myself to take very good care of Debra. My inner strength is knowing that I give God the praise and glory. One morning, I was inspired to write myself a "I Am Too Blessed To Be Stressed" list.

The list kept getting longer and longer. I now keep those blessings in a spiral notebook. I want to share just a few samples of what appeared on my list, because every process kept unfolding new discoveries for me. I would record daily in my gratitude and blessing list. It was a stressful and hostile work environment, but I managed to find comfort and healing in reading this spiral notebook in the morning before work and when I would pull out this spiral notebook from my briefcase in the afternoon for reassurance. For me, repetitions in hearing these words became my affirmations. Here are a few examples:

I am a valuable employee

I am healthy

I am confident

I am smart

I am a caring person

I am a beautiful woman

I am happy to be Herman and Gloria Washington's loving daughter

I am proud to be Joseph's mother

I am happy in my union with Joe

I am a respectable and approachable person

I am happy to be gainfully employed
I am thankful for our lovely home and safe
environment
I am learning new skills to startup my business
I am active in my church
I am volunteering my time in the community to serve
and help others
I am a friendly person

Before I even realized it, those negative people in the workplace existed but they no longer bothered me. They didn't change but, I did. I was so pumped up and charged up, it amazed them. They could not rattle me. I no longer surrendered my leadership or control to others.

The next process was viewing the things I had successfully accomplished throughout my life. I just picked an increment of a 15 year span. I would jot down my accomplishments and read this regularly. There were days when a major milestone slipped at work and I would take it personal. There were others on the team and their input would be slow in completing a project. I knew I must let it go, the stress was building up. My point is simply this: If I could find a way to motivate myself to spring back into action, then, so can others. So, why not share my story and message.

We all have those days when you are hard on yourself and in a slump. I developed this accomplishment log, just as a reminder that I have successfully achieved many things in life. You have to just pick

thoughts out of your system. Start now to rebuild your spirit. It will anchor your soul. Start jotting down your accomplishments. You will discover the positive mechanisms inside you which will transform your life. Turn your fears, resentment and anger into hope and develop a "can do" attitude. You will find inside you, a hidden treasure chest, that is filled with silver and gold. Earlier, I told you about writing a time span by increments. So, get busy now. Here are examples of some of those specific things:

Birth to 15 --What I have accomplished:
* Graduated from kindergarten
* Pageant queen in elementary school
* Graduated from sixth grade
* Maintained decent grades in elementary and junior high school
* Meeting new school mates every year
* Participated in the Future Business Leadership Program in high school

Age 15 to 30 years
* Graduated from senior high school
* Captain of the cheerleading squad at George Washington Carver Senior High School during my 10th, 11th and 12th grade years
* Worked part-time in the Accounting Department at New Orleans Parish School Board
* Financed 100% of my college education

- ❖ Pledged and proud to be affiliated with Alpha Kappa Alpha Sorority
- ❖ Received a Bachelor of Science Degree in Accounting from Southern University at New Orleans
- ❖ Happily married at 21 years of age to Mr. Joseph Gould, Jr.
- ❖ A proud and loving mother to Joseph Gould, III
- ❖ A loving daughter of Herman and Gloria Washington
- ❖ A loving daughter in law of Fannie and Joe Gould, Sr.
- ❖ Earned Master's of Science Degree in Management, Florida Institute of Technology
- ❖ Started my first professional career job
- ❖ Started my own business at 33 years old as a Professional Speaker, Trainer and Consultant
- ❖ Exercise regularly 3 to 4 days week
- ❖ Eat healthy foods
- ❖ Setting and achieving annual goals
- ❖ Living my life with a meaningful purpose
- ❖ Homeowner
- ❖ Starting frequent vacation traveling with my adorable family
- ❖ Networking, creating, building and developing meaningful friendships and relationships
- ❖ Attending regular bible study and church
- ❖ Enjoying family time
- ❖ Every week reading a good book for motivation and growth

Age 30to 45 years

- ❖ Published Author
- ❖ Still growing as a person every day
- ❖ Continue to be happily married and enriching my marriage life with Joseph Gould, Jr.
- ❖ Continue to be a loving, caring and nurturing mother to Joseph Gould, III
- ❖ Appreciating and watching our teenager grow into his own identity
- ❖ Preparing the next generation for college life
- ❖ Continue to incorporate physical fitness into my daily regiment
- ❖ Continuing bible study

Once I started this process, I realized the next process. I was no longer focusing on the negativity and hurtful words expressed by others in the workplace. You know the ones who would try to rock your world in a mean spirited way. I am wearing my shield of "To Love, Serve and Protect" Debra. Of course, I heard their words but they had no meaning at all or power. I didn't give it attention, anymore.

The next process I discovered was that you don't have to be "An Extra In Somebody Else's Play." People are fully aware of the choice of words used to attack and hurt you. It's only when they are caught that they become apologetic. If you step back and observe people, its really their own suffering and pain. It has nothing to do

with you. Some are trying to divert their attention, maybe away from their own misery and problems at others expense. But, I do not buy into this at all. I would extend myself to help a person but never allowing myself to be abused or used by manipulation, games and deceptions. If you chose not to allow their words into your mind, they will have no power. By accident, I discovered this unknown secret from a relative. This person tried so hard to get me upset over something trivial. She repeated the remarks. I made a conscious effort to ignore her with no response. I later found out that she was having problems in her marriage. A smile on my face brought more unhappiness to her. She would pick and pick at me, for no apparent reason. She would have the nerve to say, "Didn't you hear what I said to you?" Again, I just ignored her. Several weeks later in a different setting, she tried to bring the subject matter up again. I watched this person in total frustration, trying to force an argument about trivial stuff. You've heard the old saying "it takes two to argue." This was the perfect illustration. She had no one to fuss with, and she couldn't provoke me to fuss. I had reached a maturity level and I didn't have to argue. I started incorporating this unique discovery into my workplace and noticed, it really works. Most people are very aware and conscious of the things they say to you. Its only after you correct them about something or challenge their negative conversation that their reply usually is "I'm so sorry, you misunderstood me. I meant no harm." My point is, I've stopped entertaining and feeding on negativity.

The lessons learned are to be focused and to become aware of

your own uniqueness. Start unleashing the power sources inside you. Realize you have the potential to grow spiritually as a person. Realize that even in our stressful moments, we can find blessings in reaching out to help others, share with others, learn from others, and believe in others and yourself. You cannot escape negativity and negative people but you control your actions. Lastly, see the good in every day, even in the midst of trials and tribulation. They too, will come to pass.

Debra Washington Gould, MS
New Orleans, LA.

Good Fortune

$\mathcal{I}$t is my good fortune to be asked to contribute to this *Sisters Together* series by one of the authors, Debra Washington Gould. In fact, throughout my life I have been most fortunate.

My life choices, like everyone's, have often been in response to circumstances and situations that have taken me from my birthplace in New Iberia, Louisiana to Athens, Greece, and many places in between. Something happened several years ago that made me realize that although I may be fortunate, I really am responsible for my own good fortune.

One evening, I went to an Oriental restaurant with some friends. After dinner, we all got fortune cookies and my cookie was empty. That had never happened to any of us before, so I asked for another cookie and got another one - another one with no fortune inside.

My comment at the time was, "It only goes to show you that we make our own fortunes." And I did not take another cookie. I have thought about that often and have told this story many times

since then.   That event really changed my outlook.

Just this past Christmas my youngest sister, with whom I shared this story, gave me a gold fortune cookie pendant, hanging from a silk cord - with a permanent fortune inside - one that reflects my philosophy about life - one that I would like to share with you.

"To enjoy the full flavor of life, always take big bites."

Perhaps, you too, will get a message from my experience, or even from a fortune cookie that will be meant just for you in your life. This thought is something on which to reflect and remember as you make many of life's choices. I call it one of life's little, big lessons. Yes, it is my good fortune - to be sharing this with you. After all is said and done, I still do not believe in luck, but rather, that we make our own good fortunes. Go for it!

Arlene LeBlanc Broussard
Lafayette, LA

Coping

*H*ow do we cope with a man? Husband, Lover, Son, Brother, who has become all consumed by drugs and/or alcohol?

Many females, feel it's their fault or as a deserter; therefore, you say to yourself, "Hang in there, that's my (Husband, Lover, Son or Brother), and he needs me."

That is the question. How *does* he need you?

To be strong, to continually feed his dependence by making sure he does not hit rock bottom. By holding him up, in spite of the humiliation you both experience. In spite of the fact that you are the only one maintaining a roof over his head. In spite of the fact that you are constantly in jeopardy of losing your job due to stress, restless nights and tension. Therefore, you miss work or don't perform at your best.

Strength, Dear Sister, is not the scenario you just read. Strength is hanging in by demonstrating, constantly, Tough Love!

Lois Gould-Ford
New Orleans, LA

I Understand

I understand space to gather ones thoughts. But, how difficult it can be, waiting for those thoughts to formulate.

I understand it takes patience to cultivate a good relationship. But, how difficult it can be, waiting for the seed to flower.

I understand that I should not ponder, extensively. But how difficult it can be, waiting for all to materialize.

I understand caring and loving are bitter-sweet emotions that go into a relationship. But, how difficult it can be, waiting for the bitter to return to sweet.

I also understand the old saying, "Good things come to those who wait." Oh, how difficult it can be, waiting for that "Good Thing."

Lois Gould-Ford
New Orleans, LA

Just Say Yes!

*A*shley is a Girl Scout!

It may not seem remarkable to you that a thirteen year old is a Girl Scout, but let me tell you the story.

When Ashley was in third grade, I called the local Brownie leader and said, "I would like my daughter to be in scouting, but there are some things you might need to know. Ashley was born with a smooth brain, causing severe mental and medical problems. She uses a wheelchair, has no speech, wears diapers, has seizures, and is fed through a tube in her stomach."

Holding my breath, I asked, "So, what do you think?"

Kelly just said, "Yes, Girl Scouts are for all girls and of course Ashley is welcome."

Fifteen minutes later, Kelly called back. "I'm scared to death," she said. "I've never been around a child like Ashley. I don't know what to do."

I told her to continue doing what she already had done. Just say "yes." Continue to model acceptance and openness as she already

had when she accepted Ashley into the troop.

Ashley's scouting career began. At the first meeting Ashley had show and tell. All the girls sat in a wide circle around her. I said, "You can see how Ashley is different. Let's talk about how she is the same."

They asked, "What does she do for fun? How does she communicate?" With each answer, they got closer and closer to her. Soon they were right up on her, touching and caressing her. For the most part their fears were gone.

They learned that Ashley enjoyed bubble baths, music, people, and riding on the back of my bike. She communicates by smiling and turning toward the person talking to her.

The session lasted ten minutes longer than scheduled. Who says children are cruel? It has been my experience that if you help them to understand the situation, they are very accepting. Most of the girls just said "yes" to Ashley.

During one exercise at the meeting, the girls were supposed to break into groups of three and note something they had in common and something that was different about them.

Ashley was having a seizure at this time. Her little face was red, she was drooling, and she was not a pretty sight. When Kelly got to their group, she asked, "What was the same?" A little girl replied, "We all wear jewelry."

Kelly looked over at me and held her breath when she asked, "What was different?" The little girl said, "I'm 8, she is 7 1/2, and Ashley is 7."

Having a seizure was just part of being Ashley. They accepted her for who she was.

Ashley is now a Cadet Scout. We have gone on field trips, sold cookies and spent weekends camping. Girls of all ages have interacted with Ashley. Some have come to me and said, "You know, Ms. Sharyn, we are all different, and it is okay to be different."

Ashley is a teacher. She is teaching that diversity is good, that we all have gifts to share, and that we benefit when we just say "yes" to each other.

Sharyn Scheyd
Kenner, LA

Grief & Strength

I was as most women are, a "Daddy's girl." My father could do no wrong and he spoiled me, completely. What I loved most about my father is that unlike my mother he was still alive after I passed my rebel stage. My mother unfortunately passed away when I was twenty years old, still a rebel and at an age when I did not fully appreciate my parents.

A child grows in various stages, from dependency, independence, rebellion, and finally, interdependence. My father and I had reached the stage of interdependence and a fondness for one another. I saw my father as my buddy. Whenever I went out, whether to the store or to dinner, I would invite him. I also wanted to protect my father from my brothers who only saw him as a cook, a bank, or a ride. My father and I were just like roommates. It was just the two of us in the house (after the passing of my aunt), we both loved and respected one another.

In July of 1993, my aunt passed away and it made me realize that I may soon lose my father. From that moment on I would call

him each day during my lunch period just to say, "Hi." If he did not answer, I was on my way home to make sure he was okay. Well, on a Friday in March of 1994 my father called me at 10:30 a.m. to tell me he had to run some errands and would probably not be home during my lunch time. He ended the call by telling me that he loved me and I told him I loved him too. The rest of the day went as usual and when I arrived home at 5:30 p.m., I unfortunately found my father in his bed. As I walked in the room I knew he was already gone, I touched his toe, and he was ice cold. For some strange reason I called the ambulance and started pacing in front of the house. I had no idea what to do. At that very moment, my boyfriend now husband, Dominic Hornsby, called me, just to talk. The weird thing was that his schedule normally keeps him busy until late. However, that day he came home early and called me. We talked later about this day and he indicated he didn't know what came over him, but when he laid his head down, he had the sudden urge to call me.

For most of the next few of days, I was a basket case. Arrangements had to be made, burial deeds has to found; so much to do in a little time. My father passed away on a Friday. The next morning my mothers' first cousin decided to pay us a visit to request the burial deeds for my mother's family plot. We could not find them; therefore, she left empty-handed. I had no idea that she could have had that much hate and prejudice in her heart, that she would not allow my father to be buried where both his wife and two sons were buried (my mother's first cousin was a very fair skin black woman, and my father was by contrast, much darker than her).

Unfortunately, I could not deal with this crisis at the time, other things were more pressing.

The following Monday when we arrived at the cemetery, the director informed us that without the cemetery deeds we could not bury my father in the plot because of the wishes of mother's first cousin. Prior to the director making this statement, I was crying, but, at that moment, I realized that strength was needed to make decisions. I composed myself and began to assess the situation. The director indicated that another family plot could be purchased for $10,000. I indicated that this was not acceptable. My sister was actually considering this purchase, but I quickly reminded her that the full financial responsibility would rest solely on the two daughters and that the three sons would not put up their respective shares. When we arrived at the funeral home, we found a solution that was both feasible and financially possible.

The weeks following my father's death were both painful and exhausting. I had the dubious task of going through all the paper work to close out debt and assets that remained. My siblings took the financially uneducated attitude that, if he was dead, the debt would be dissolved. I realized that if we were to inherit my parent's house we would also inherit any liabilities.

My father was my friend and buddy who passed away nine months before my wedding date, November 19, 1994. I would have loved to have him walk me down the aisle, but it wasn't to be. My father died the way he wanted to, in his sleep in his bed, not in a hospital hooked up to machines. Sometimes, I wonder if I had come

home during that day in March, 1994, could I have saved him? Would I have made it home in time for medical personnel to resuscitate him, bring him to a hospital where he might have died in a couple of days, weeks, or months, who knows? But, what I do know is that my father looked as though he was at peace. He was on his way home to see his wife, and other ancestors that had passed on before him.

Barbara A. Eveque-Hornsby, CPA
New Orleans, LA

Family Values and Math:
A Study in Probability

$\mathcal{T}$he phone rings over and over, bearing news of this Aunt or another. But of course, weather reports and forecasts always precede any real news when we get these calls from our family in Nebraska. The typical response to such tidbits of information is to acknowledge them with remarks like, "Oh dear," "Not again!" or "Oh, really?" This particular call, though, turned more quickly than usual to news about a childhood friend. My interest intensified as my mother recited recent events.

You see, this friend's Grandparents knew my Grandparents. They farmed the good, rich earth only miles apart from one another. In fact, both set of ancestors helped build the German speaking school a few miles away from their farm. You know the one you reach by walking a couple of miles, through freezing, driving snow? Well, this was the one my own mother taught in, complete with wooden floors that were swept daily and had a coal burning stove that needed stoking at night. Next to the stove was a coal bin, well stocked by the farmers in the vicinity. More than once I heard the story about the

black snakes that liked to nest, deep in the recesses of that coal bin. Yes, that old stand by, fossil fuel, would warm the school room before the students arrived.

As time passed, the old homestead was sold, and my parents moved to the capitol city of Nebraska, believe it or not, on the very same street, as the friend my mother was phoning about. As a child, I watched with a little envy and longing as this friend built go-carts, forts, and hide-outs with any small left over pieces of wood he could find. His parents had started a contracting business and bits of scrap wood and building materials had become a routine resource in his life. He eventually joined the family business as it prospered through German persistence and frugality, building shopping malls, motels, and apartment buildings all over the state. Always, his family worked side by side, doing their best. After all, that was expected. They learned together to practice their art. They saw themselves and their lives as important. They interacted together like intricately-woven threads in a finely designed piece of cloth. And they instinctively knew the probability formula for success, the same method that large corporations now advocate, and great schools emulate. That old fashioned wisdom says people on the same side work as a team, keeping agreed-upon goals in mind. Spice it up with taking time out to care about each other, and you have a sure recipe for prosperity.

The probability of my friend's family being successful was high. No one in the community doubted it, particularly the members of this family who toiled endlessly but, happily together. For after all, if something needed to be done, you did it. Neither age nor gender

were concerns. Accomplishing your goals and achieving your shared visions, those were the issues.

To this day, my friend's parents haven't moved from the house they bought thirty some years ago. A probability study likely would have predicted that, too. Their business dreams were more important than keeping up with those legendary Jones'.

Anyway, the news on the telephone that day was that my friend, now in his mid-forties, had fallen thirty feet off a scaffolding and crushed the left side of his body, leg, hip, and arms. After his hospital stay, he moved to a rehabilitation home. His mother faithfully drives over in the afternoon and again after dinner to take him things, but mostly just to be there. The doctors have spoken words in the sometimes sterile, unbending language of math. "There is a possibility he may not walk again, a probability his gait will have an unnatural rhythm, a pronounced limp." The doctors' hypothetical theories do not agree with the family's probability belief. The stalwart Nebraska family remains unshaken. According to his mother, these words are just that, talk, floating in the air like breath on a cold winter morning. "This fellow has tremendous will, and a steady constitution" says his brother. The family knows the real probability is that he'll be up and walking by spring. In fact, they all talk about what a good thing it is that this happened in the winter months when construction is slow, so he'll have plenty of time to recuperate before the frost thaws and the dogwood trees bud.

Oh, how you wish as a teacher you could compress this farm-value determination into a sugar coated vitamin pill to hand to your

students every morning with their daily language assignment.

Without mentioning my friend's father, this study wouldn't be complete. He has withstood two triple by-pass surgeries in the last several years. He still manages to visit as many of the family's building cites as time allows each day. His probability verdict concerning his son's recovery is still out. He couldn't be reached for comment. He was out at the country home his with son, wife, and three children. There he was, putting the final touches on a wooden ramp for his son to use to get up the stairs, until he could be back out there, walking on his own, come Spring,

Barbara J. Cypher, M.Ed.
Riyadh, Saudi Arabia

Then & Now

Although the thirty years of my life which the Master has blessed me with have been filled with situations and decisions, I don't think that I would have planned it any differently. When I was in what I consider my pre-adult state, there were many questions that I had that I didn't know whether I would ever get answered. On my many confused days, I would ask the Master what was the real purpose for this precious gift of life, He'd given to me. Now that I have grown to be a responsible adult, I think I know some of the answers, but not all of them.

Responsibility, as I knew it Then, was only concerns of myself, Now true responsibilities are concerns for myself, my daughter, my husband, in addition to family and friends.

Everything was me, me, me....that was, Then. Now, everything is we, and our. Realizing that as long as my fist was balled up, I couldn't give anything, nor could I receive anything. It is so much easier excepting the fact that it's o.k. not to be able to do everything on your own.

All I had was me, which I thought brought so much joy to this world....that was, Then. Now, as a result of my daughter, true joy has been given to me. My daughter relies on me to love, support, teach her moral and spiritual values and protect her. After all, I was told that a wife is suppose to be submissive to her husband. I couldn't agree with this...that was Then. Now, I would agree that we both should be submissive to one another on every level.

What I remember then, was having the helping hand from my mother and father through their love and support, only for me to reject it, by being unappreciative and not showing gratitude. I was selfish and I thought outside people knew what was better for me, more so, than my parents. So, I guess this is a good time to apologize to my parents for ever doubting them. A helping hand only enhances what is already there. Understanding and appreciation of family was something I vaguely remembered,then. Now, I realize these understandings are the most precious blessings that the Master has given to me.

Ah...True friendship on my part, was my top priority...that was then. Now, true friendship still exists, except it's from a distance. The main lesson learned about these friendships was that all of them were held together because I was the one who treated these individuals like relatives, only to be reminded they weren't. These shallow friendships demonstrated to me that they had no true loyalty to me. Loyalty was what I expected of them, but I didn't receive this. After confiding in each friend, the pattern was the same, that is, we would grow distant from each other once I stopped giving tangible things. It has taken me

a long time to accept the fact that I had to be less, in order to make them more. In order to make them comfortable with our relationship, I did things to boost their moral and reduce my own, so that they could shine brighter...that was, then. Now, in order to maintain a friendship with me the rule is, I will except you as you are, what you are and what you stand for, and in return, you do the same for me.

I used to be very confused about my life's decisions...that was then. Now, because of faith, I have a blue print for what my life purpose is. There have been many situations which have helped to shape the person I am today. Blowing up, not thinking things through and acting out...that was, then. Now I listen, I rationalize and make the appropriate decision. Taking chances was second nature to me...that was Then. Now, I'm very aware of the circumstance and all persons involved.

Sometimes, I find myself overwhelmed and again wondering what is happening in my life. After a talk with myself, I realized that the person who can make the changes is me, because I want it that way. I used to block out dealing with situations by keeping busy doing frivolous things...that was Then. Now, I approach situations head on, without fear, because either way it goes, I will still have to deal with it. Allowing people to use me financially, as well as, manipulating me...that was, then. Now, I'm conscious of my financial situation and although I am generous to family members, it is only during their times of essential need that I offer my assistance.

What I have realized now, is that my gift of listening, understanding and helping individuals to find their own solutions, is

greater than anything that I could ever offer them. It is a wonderful feeling when you have accomplished a goal or goals on your own, although someone assisted you, by giving guidance...LESSON LEARNED!

Sheree T. Venson-Nelson
New Orleans, LA

Piercing The Armor

On October 16, 1997, I learned that I would once again have to face a vicious and formidable foe. This can't be real! It's been a year in October that my family did battle with this enemy. Will I lose this time? My mind filled with rage and grief as I revisit the scenes from my last battle.

It was late August, 1996 when I received a call from my younger sister, Lois. "Momma is not doing too well, the doctor found additional carcinoma behind her nose." The family had been on a two year emotional roller coaster and it was down again. The end of September brought good news, they were able to get to the cancer and remove it. One week after Momma's operation, my mother, my rock was beginning to give way. Fannie's children were called together by the physician who informed us that Momma's condition was terminal, and she would not last two months. The cancer had invaded her liver and her now frail body would not survive the necessary treatment. The doctor indicated that he was unable to do any more for our mother. He indicated that she was a very proud and

dignified woman and it would not serve her to let her die in a hospital. We all agreed. She agreed, she wanted to be with her family.

The big question for the family was, how do we take care of a caretaker? We basically tried to make her as comfortable as possible, but her body was rapidly relinquishing its power. Her mind still in tact, she tried to no avail to continue to do things for herself. I needed to convince her to let us take care of her. She fought back our efforts to help her. She didn't want to be a burden. She was not ready to surrender her self-reliance.

How was I to pierce the armor that Momma wore to protect herself from emotional slumps, despair, blame, and resentment? How could I penetrate the armor that hid from her children her personal suffering? She fought her battles alone, took care of her own. Her physical strength was gone, she could no longer live with her commitment to herself to take care of her children. How can I serve her, be there for her and allow her to keep the one thing she had left, her dignity? Questions, questions, I was drowning in the need to know. I had lived in the same discourse as my mother for most of my adult life. How could I? I needed an answer. I laid close to momma, looked past the frailness and into her eyes. There, I found what she was asking for. The words seemed to flow from her eyes like musical notes. "Let me take care of you." I realized that I still needed her help, I couldn't do this alone. I needed her to walk with me through this unfamiliar place. "Please momma, take care of me. Take care of me by allowing me to serve you. I need this. You have always given

and taken care of me. Allow me to have that experience with you." The frailness of my mother's face shifted into a weak smile. She has surrendered.

Learning to live with integrity, by bearing the truth of my experience allows me to cultivate virtues like honesty, humility, courage, diligence, and discernment that hold me in good stead when an inevitable interruption in my life occurs.

The lesson learned that night was openness. No more confusion, no more fear. Doing it myself, doesn't mean I do it independently of others' support. In being open to what I hold as true, I am able to touch others with a spirit of authenticity that opens invitations of support and commitment.

Thank you momma, for taking care of me. In my battle with the enemy, my lessons have served me. The universe is friendly. Unfolding continually for me is an abiding faith in God, support, a continued flow of needed information, prayer, love, gratitude, and strength in knowing that I will win. I have pierced the armor.

Pamela Sherrard, ODC/MS
Gonzales, LA

"With Bullets of Determination"

"*I* am a polio survivor, I hope that is politically correct because I have gone from crippled to disabled to differently abled. Pretty soon, I'll be cured."

Forty years later, I can joke about my disability, even as a "sit up comedian" but when I was eight years old, polio turned my life upside down. It was a very cruel joke that was anything but funny.

In the small farming community in Minnesota where I grew up, life was taken very seriously. One bad storm could wipe out a crop my father had planned for, and had physically nurtured for months. One bad virus did the same for me. Early in life, however, my family planted the seeds of hard work, perseverance, and simple living deep within my soul. These values have helped many accomplishments take root for me, over the course of my life.

Before polio (BP) I was only aware of my immediate world which was bitter/sweet, and mostly sweet. After polio (AP) my life was primarily bitter . . . for ten long years. From the time I contracted polio until I left home for college, I lived in a world of inner darkness and anguish. This was due in part to my belief system at the time which was there was no hope for me. Making my life a productive meaningful existence, without the full use of my legs was an impossibility. In my hometown, few women went to college. Our culture said men and women were stewards of the earth, and college

did not necessarily fit that model. However, as I approached high school graduation, I was aware of a quiet yearning to do something to compensate for the loss of the use of my legs.

With the support of my family and many others close to me, the possibility of college became a reality and at that point, a new life began for me. Ten years after my legs became paralyzed, my entry into college helped me shake the paralysis in my mind (i.e. my negative beliefs).

In the fall of my eighteenth year, I left the land of "milk and cornfields" to begin my college career. Compared to my experiences in the small town of Bird Island, Minnesota - life in the big city of St. Paul, Minnesota, one hundred miles way, was quite an adjustment. I felt like an ant on a football field.

Nevertheless, college quickly became a magical way of life. People were helpful, friendly, and non-judgmental. I felt as though I had died and went to heaven! Unfortunately, at that time, my study habits were somewhere between bad and non-existent. My scholarship required that I obtain a "C" average for the year, a feat that I accomplished my first year, but barely. You see, my first year of college could be summed up in three words, fun, fun, and fun! Studying was low on my list of priorities and yet, I was vaguely aware of the need to strive and work harder at it. My awareness did not turn into action until the fall of my sophomore year of college. Then came the infamous day- November 22, 1963. Where were you when you heard that John F. Kennedy had been shot to death in Dallas, Texas? I was in French lab listening to some kind of gibberish when the

announcement was made in English. { I wished that bad news was made in French, for I wouldn't have been able to understand it.} I was grief stricken! Deja vu - I had the same terrible feeling one morning in August when I woke up without a leg to stand on. However, the experience of a similar terrible feeling was even more profound this time.

I did not know President Kennedy personally, but I felt as though I had a deep connection with him somehow. The connection was brutally torn apart when the report of his assassination was given. In shock, all through the horrendous scenes of the assassination itself, I watched his solitary wife, his innocent children and that rider-less horse. Sometimes the cadence still echoes in my heart. President Kennedy and I were both shot down in our prime.

Nonetheless, even now I do not fully comprehend what happened to me subsequently. Like many other things, it may not be necessary to understand. Today, I call what happened to me, inspiration. Then, I called it -desperation! Both can be great mot-ivators.

I was greatly affected by President John F. Kennedy, more in his death than in his life. It was an inspired state that lasted the rest of my college years. Immediately, I began to study his life and I dedicated myself to having the same vision he had. Then, I began to study day and night, just as I thought he would have done, if he were me. After that, I focused on nothing but my education. I was determined to excel just as he had done. I sat in the library seven days a week, seven to ten hours every day to enrich my knowledge and to

develop my power of concentration.

In President Kennedy's honor, I dedicated myself to excellence and to fully utilizing my talents whenever and wherever the opportunity presented itself. Characteristically, I even named my wheelchair after President Kennedy's PT Boat: PT 109. I was determined to avoid sinking into despair and mediocrity ever, ever again - and I have not.

Now, many years have passed since my college years. As my daughter begins her college career, I am again reminded of those mystifying college years. Once again, I marvel at the wonder of those days and the inspiration that I experienced that propelled me ever onward. Despite being a disabled woman, having been raised in a small farming community where college was neither expected nor advocated, I began to soar instead of feel sorry for myself. This was also long before the Americans with Disability Act legislation was enacted, which has brought forth fewer physical obstacles to overcome. Yet, despite the odds against me, somehow I was able to remold my life, with the help of my God and attend graduate school in social work and have a wonderful, fulfilling life - helping myself and others, overcome obstacles in life.

My philosophy is to *Use What You've Got To Make Your Life Better* and to *Help Others Do The Same*. When I do "sit up comedy" in my speaking career and when in my personal life I work with my two children to use what they've got. I often smile to myself in deep admiration for the awesome power of the human spirit. Better use of my legs, oh yes, that would be wonderful.

 Better use of my mind, heart, and spirit, oh yes, that has made my life so much better! We can all do it by using what we've got and planting new seeds that help us grow and soar to ever new heights.

Marion Wikholm MSW, BCSW
Metairie, LA

Order That Pizza!

I realized that returning to the workplace after about a twelve year absence would indeed be an adjustment. There had been many changes in the office environment during that decade. Computers had replaced typewriters, the telephone had changed from a normal sized desk telephone with a few buttons at the bottom, to an enormous instrument empowered to answer itself and relay messages. It was all very intimidating but the excitement of my work gave me the momentum to get pass the various obstacles.

I remember so well that first challenge! After being introduced to many of my future coworkers and getting my desk area in order, I began working furiously on my initial assignment. Before I knew it, it was lunch time and I was starving. The culture of the office seemed to be brown bag lunches. Most of the office staff had brought lunch from home. The few that left the office did not mention having me join them. I was in a strange part of our city and was not sure where I could go for lunch. Additionally, I had a lot to do and really needed to work throughout the lunch hour.

There was a solution, however. I would simply order a pizza and eat it at my desk. I reached for the complicated looking telephone and dialed the number of a local pizza place (I knew it well, as the parent of teenagers). When I heard . . . Hello . . . Yes . . . What is it . . . and many such greetings, I thought to myself how anxious the Pizza Place must be for my business that day. I responded appropriately, "May I have a pepperoni pizza with extra cheese, please?" There was a strange silence, but I proceeded to give the address of my office and my name. Another strange silence...and then the receptionist came on the line and said, "Mary Kay, you hit the intercom button and you are speaking to every executive in the building." I learned later, I was also speaking to the entire lunch room.

While I did not get a pizza that day, I did come to know absolutely everyone in the office. Someone from the lunchroom came into my work area laughing hysterically and invited me to share her lunch. Others from all areas of the organization dropped by to chuckle with me about my very embarrassing incident. Before I went home that day there were many things I had learned. No doubt, the two most important were how to operate the telephone system and the fact that I had been blessed with an outstanding group of co-workers! The humorous, though embarrassing event, had created an instant bond.

My ill fated order for pizza earned me an opportunity to laugh with my new good friends. In my life, I depend a lot on humor...in fact, it is ranked right up there with food and shelter. Breaking down

the sense of distance that occurs naturally between managers and those they supervise can often be done with a sense of humor. It is easier to trust someone with whom we can share a good laugh than someone who appears distant. We had created a humor/trust circle and cemented a work relationship of mutual confidence and good will.

As the years went by, like every organization we had times when the workload was overwhelming. Often, when things were going wrong, someone would point to me and say, "Mary Kay, would you please order a pizza today? We need a good laugh!"

Mary Kay Kurzweg
Metairie, LA

"Kick the Ladder Away
Live Your Dreams and
Just Do It"

"*Y*ou are the only person I know who follows her dreams. When you set your goals, you just implement them, right away. When you say you're going to do it, you just do it." I am always amazed at the feedback I receive from what I consider, doing what comes naturally. I've always wanted to be different and to make a contribution. My brother tells me that's where I get my energy.

About two years ago, after the death of my father, I was working as a Public Relations person for the U.S. Department of Energy. My duties included "meeting and greeting" at various public events. The event which changed my life was during "Public Service Recognition Week."

A scientist from the United States Department of Agriculture (USDA) who had previously done volunteer work for me, came up to my booth and asked me what I was doing now. I was at a crossroads in life trying to decide what I was going to be when I grow up. Having been an attorney for 20 years and a public relations specialist, I had skills. I had been visiting small manufacturing companies and taking courses at a local community college on manufacturing. I was the only woman, lawyer, and African American attending the conference. I told my scientist-friend, "I think I'll be a lawyer again," concentrating on governmental relations or lobbying instead of doing

something I did not know anything about.

My scientist told me "That would be a mistake." I asked him "What do you have in mind?" He told me about patents that scientists at the USDA develop. Many good food products, but no one takes them to market. A light bulb went on in my head. I was intimately familiar and involved with agricultural research because my daddy, a Ph.D. animal scientist, was the scientist that discovered how to reduce cholesterol in eggs and pork. This was his major research in the 1970s. Of course, I knew about agricultural research. I did not know, however, how to take a product to market. I asked the scientist if he would help me. He agreed. Consequently, I began the process of developing a team of experts to help me bring the products my scientist developed to market. In October 1997, I left my government career with 15 years of service to devote 100 percent of my efforts to bringing healthy rice-based snacks to market.

Cleopatra Foods is now my full-time job. "How did you decide to name your company, Cleopatra Foods?" you may ask. My oral surgeon and friend, on a visit to his office gave me a compliment on the pair of earrings I was wearing. "Durinda, I like your earrings." I thanked him and wondered what about these earrings reminded him of Cleopatra.

I could have taken the compliment on a superficial level and thought he's flirting big time and he thinks I'm cute. I knew, however, that he was also a scholarly type. So, I decided to conduct research to see what characteristics of Cleopatra he saw in me.

My research included everything I could read on Cleopatra. I

even rented the 1963 film version of "Cleopatra," starring, Elizabeth Taylor. I watched every frame of this four-hour movie, looking for clues. The earrings were shaped like a statue in New York and London called "Cleopatra Needle." I discovered that Cleopatra was an intelligent, charming, witty, and nurturing woman who was also very ambitious. This research helped me discover who I really am.

She is known by her two famous relationships, Julius Caesar and Mark Anthony. I studied the lives of these two men and their relationship with Cleopatra. Her relationship with Mark Anthony was the most popular, but the relationship with Julius Caesar was the healthier one. Julius Caesar made Cleopatra rich by establishing trade between Egypt and Rome. One of the products was rice. I wondered if my friend was putting me to a test. I wondered if I'm Cleopatra, are you Julius Caesar? Thereafter, I called him Caesar, and I attributed his "nickname" as being an inspiration and motivating force in my life.

Cleopatra Foods is now in the business development stage. Everyday someone comes along my path to help me along the way. Recently, the president of the venture capitalist fund I have been dealing with told me that she's been hearing all about Cleopatra Foods, and told them to give that woman some money. Alright!

Durinda L. Robinson
New Orleans, LA

The Reunion

I received a phone call one morning, early in January of 1997. The caller was my sister Ali, who happened to work as a nurse and lived just around the corner. She stated that our sister Marie was hospitalized and had been diagnosed with cancer. This news forever changed my life. Both my sister and mother had been informed of this devastating news days before. Marie, however, did not want me to know. You must understand, we had a relationship that was on and off for many years, depending upon many factors. If she was a having a good financial year, it was on. When I had successes in my career, purchased my home, the relationship was off. Various events and circumstances shaped our relationship, causing it to be strained and unhealthy.

Ali and I continued our conversation regarding Marie's condition. Her cancer was discovered in the liver and she would require chemotherapy to possibly lengthen her life. She also needed a place to live, and both my mother and Ali were unable to accommodate her in their homes. I was asked to take her in, since I lived alone, with my dog Missey. I had loads of space.

The moment I knew of her condition, was the moment I knew I would offer her residence in my home to assist with her recovery. You see, I had practiced as a nurse for 20 years, prior to a career change.

I visited Marie in the hospital that same afternoon and found her frail, frightened and quite ill. She was surprised to see me, but welcomed my visit. It was a challenge to control my emotions during the visit. Having cared for cancer patients in the past, I knew the impact it would have on her body and her mental well-being. She was going to require a lot of care, just to get her physically able to tolerate chemotherapy.

Marie accepted my offer and plans were made to discharge her within the next couple of days. Meanwhile, I discussed with Ali and Mother the level of support they could provide since being a business owner would make this task of care giver even more of a challenge.

For the next three weeks, care was taken in providing Marie three meals per day at the same schedule she received while hospitalized, making certain that she and I ate together eating the same foods. As she became stronger, so did our relationship. We began to laugh together as we reminisced childhood events and discussed the strategies on how to beat her cancer. It was like a reunion, and we both had joined together to fight a deadly enemy. The primary objective was to increase her quality of life as much as possible during the remainder of time left.

Marie decided against taking chemotherapy, but wanted to treat her illness with natural foods, herbs and vitamin supplements. Marie was becoming stronger and was now able prepare some meals for herself and do laundry. We thought we were winning the battle. By April, Marie announced she wanted to be in her own apartment and decided to leave against our protests. We knew she wasn't ready

physically, but I also felt under the circumstances, she should not be denied her independence.

By the middle of May, we knew she could no longer live alone. Her condition had deteriorated and she required 24 hour nursing care. Following a family discussion she was admitted to a nursing home. This decision was very difficult for her. She lashed out at me in anger, for not letting her remain in her home. Marie did not have the financial resources available for in-home care, and the family was also unable to provide assistance. After Marie spent a few days in the nursing home and was fairly settled, I went to visit her. As I walked through the door and approached her, her face lit up with a big smile and she reached for me with open arms. I knew then, the reunion continued and would never be broken in spite of death. It was difficult to see her slowly slip away from us, and I was no longer able to control my emotions during my shift at her bedside. It was oh, so painful, not to be able to prevent her from suffering. At the end, she would only let me provide her nourishment and I took comfort in knowing that she trusted and needed me to be with her. I told her I loved her and was glad that I could be there for her. My sister Marie was laid to rest June 26, 1997.

Willie R. Haywood
Cincinnati, OH

"When Life Deals You A Lemon, Get Up, Because You Can Make it"

*L*ife is short,

Life is so real,

Life is full of sunshine and sometimes filled with tears,

Life is here today and gone to become yet another tomorrow,

Life is sometimes filled with tear stained sorrow.

What can I say about this life of mine?

Lets start from the beginning. I had a rather good childhood, although I was spoiled, but not selfish or self-centered. As far as I can remember, I always had goals set in my life. First, elementary and middle school, then high school and finally college. When you are used to having your life planned ahead it can throw you for a loop, when all of a sudden you have no plans.

I can remember deciding on a Wednesday, the year was 1977, to move from Indiana to Georgia. When I arrived in Georgia with my black and white T.V., $500.00 in cash, and no job, and a car note, somehow I knew that everything was going to be alright. However, I had my recreational drug use and I was controlling it, and not

allowing it to control me. I do remember, however, for every relationship I ended I would get high as a sign of finalizing the breakup. Strange as it may sound, by getting sick the next day from getting high I felt like I deserved the sickness, based on not being able to keep the relationship together.

Then I met my husband, June, 1979, while working at C&S bank. Now ladies, when you talk about avoiding a man, by then, I was a master. Years later, we dated and on May 16, 1982, we jumped the broom or shall I say we became one. This man was so sweet to me and a good provider. However, it still wasn't enough at that time to keep me happy. I turned back to the drugs, and left my husband. I left my home to go to live in a drug infested apartment with people who I felt understood my needs. Then, three months later, I realized this living arrangement was not the way I was raised or, even for me, so I went back home to my husband. I was happy for one year and then I became restless again, and turned again to my friends, pain pills, alcohol or anything I could find at that time, to get high.

Then on June 27, 1989, I starting sinking, but I still thought I had control of my life. However, I strayed from positive friends. I did not want to hear anything that went against what I was doing to keep existing in this thing call Life. I had not only professed Jesus Christ as my Savior but, somewhere along the way, I had also put my faith on the back burner. In June, 1989, I was driving my car and went to sleep behind the wheel. My car side-swiped a tree, flipped over twice and hit another tree before coming to a halt. I stayed conscious long enough for me to call on the Lord and tell the man that had witnessed

the accident, what hospital to tell them to take me to.

After my accident, I went through a total of 19 surgeries. Well, I guess by now you are thinking "Oh, My God." No, I still had not reached my bottom. Now, added to my supply of drugs was medication in the form of a needle. During one hospitalization, in a period of 6 weeks, I had over 120 pain shots. My true friends started staying away and my husband became frustrated with my actions and embarrassed.

But, Thank God, I had a friend that took me to a hospital to talk to a counselor on July 4, 1993. When I went in to talk to him he asked personal questions and said he was going to give me an I.D. number, and for 14 days I had no public contact. He turned to my friend and told her she could leave my clothes at the front door. Then, it hit me, I am trapped, so I commenced to look for a exit. I did not find a exit, but a entrance to detox.

Then, I began to travel down the road to reclaiming my life and began again, to love me. While, in the hospital, after getting over the denial and rebellion, I was able to grasp what the counselors were trying to show and tell me. First, they said when it rains, that too shall pass. Then, with the help of the Lord and the counselor, I learned to love and appreciate me. Then, last but not least, I had to realize that I was responsible for my own happiness. When all of these things came together, I realized life had dealt me a lemon but, I had learned through trials and tribulations, how to make good lemonade.

So my sisters, when you feel like you just cannot make it, try this formula:

God+Love+Peace Of Mind+Acceptance of Who You Are = Happiness. Failure is not final only a story that needs the right ending. The choice is yours!

C. Arnold
College Park, GA

Forever Overcoming Adversity

$\mathcal{A}$t an early age, I realized that there are many challenges in life that you will face. Some challenges will be enjoyable, others will be unpleasant. No matter how pleasant or unpleasant, patience, perseverance, and endurance will produce character in any situation. My mother taught me that you should put forth your best effort in anything that you are involved in. Some of her favorite statements were, "You have to be strong to last long"; "Give it your all, don't stop, and you'll make it to the top" ; "Faith is the key ,to be all that you can be."

Unfortunately, at the age of 15, I had to cope with one of the most difficult situations a human would face in life - the sudden death of my mother. At that time, my mother and I were seriously beginning to plan my future. I relied heavily, on my mother's direction. Now, I was faced with not knowing where to get my direction from. I was very scared and felt that no one would be able to provide assistance. My teachers were worried that my life would change drastically. They were concerned that I would no longer be the intelligent and respectful young lady that they had came to know. I also wondered if I would stay focused, too.

My immediate goal was to complete high school, which

would take about three more years. My teachers were right, my life changed drastically. I not only had to focus on high school, now I was faced with taking care of a family - my father and brother.

My daily schedule included going to school, cooking meals, washing clothes, cleaning the house, studying, and doing homework. Other duties I performed were grocery shopping, budgeting household expenses and paying bills. This aggressive schedule left hardly anytime for "fun." At times, I became very weary and felt abandoned and misguided. Then, I remembered that the 15 years that I spent with my mother were not just memories, they were my direction in life. Everything that she deposited in me was still there. So, instead of avoiding thoughts of my mother, I started to meditate on past conversations and events. Although, I was still faced with the same daily challenges, my life changed from difficult to enjoyable.

My goals were accomplished at the end of the three year journey. I graduated from high school. Thanks to my mother's direction, I graduated salutatorian and received several scholastic scholarships.

I thank God for my mother, and I also know that I can look to Him for direction and guidance. One of my favorite motivational statements to myself is, *"Patience, Perseverance, and Endurance exercises your faith so that you can be all that you can be."* Forever overcoming adversity has been a natural part of life.

Greta D. Jefferson
New Orleans, LA

Before The Grass
Becomes Milk

*T*here is an old adage that states " be patient,... in time, the grass becomes milk." But, what do we do before the grass becomes milk.

I was born at 2:02 on a rainy Wednesday morning. I guess you could say that from the womb, I was anxious to get here. My two older brothers were born at 12:30, a reasonable hour but, so what, they were not as excited as I was about being here. Anyway, every since I can remember I was anxious about something. When my middle brother started school, I cried, because I wanted to go, but when I finally had the opportunity to go, I cried every day because I did not want to go. You'd think that back then, I would have learned the value of waiting, but I didn't. How many times have our mothers and grandmothers told us that patience was a virtue and to be anxious for nothing? Well, I wish that I could tell you differently but I can't. What I can tell you is that when King Solomon said in the Book of Ecclesiastes that, "there is a season and a time to every purpose under heaven," the man was right. After all, he was known as the wisest man in all the world. Well, I do not have the wisdom of Solomon, but I do know the value of patience. As I am always in a rush to do something or the other, where has all this rushing gotten me? No where. I am in the place that I was destined to be in, at this time in my life. I have a purpose that I am to fulfill, but I cannot move my

purpose along at my timing but I must wait and prepare, for the time when it shall appear.

When I was in high school, I couldn't wait until I went to college. When I was in college, I couldn't wait until I got out. Always in a hurry and always going nowhere. After I graduated from college, I had to have a new car and my own place and my own furniture. Needless to say, I ended up in debt and with all the possessions that I owned, they had little value. I remember this older gentleman telling me that Rome was not built in a day, and to take it slow. I did not care about Rome or when it was built, I needed what I needed and what I needed, I wanted, right then.

At twenty-five, I was in a hurry to get married to Mr. Wrong. My best friend had been married for three years, so, to me, I was behind schedule and had to catch up. The relationship ended with me being broken-hearted. I moved to Atlanta to start a brand new life. Since I was eager to put the past behind, I started all over again. New furniture, new clothes, new hair style, new attitude, and a new car. My new life was exciting, expensive and going nowhere, fast. But, I was moving, and that was important to me. Life was too short to keep still, I had to stay in motion.

One day, all the madness stopped. I experienced a love, like I had never known before. People say that you never forget your first love, well, my first love never forgot me. In spite of all that I had done or not done, God took me back. I slowed down a bit and took time out to see where my life was going. I had to make a change. People say change is good, change enhances growth. I say change is slow.

So, even though I gave my life back to Christ, I still refused to wait for my change to come. I decided to change jobs, then I went back to school to change careers but that took too long, so I quit. At 29, I was back on the marriage kick again and ended up in the same places as the last time. But, this time I didn't move. I learned how to trust in the Lord, even in the bad times. He walked with me, and talked with me; and He told me to wait with patience, hope and courage.

Paul Masson Company's motto is, "We will sell no wine before it is time." Why was I always trying to sell to the first buyer? Because, I was always impatient. I wanted to run my life the way my friends ran theirs. Deborah was a wife and mother, I wanted that, too. Nancy had an awesome career, I wanted that too.

Through much prayer, I finally reached one plateau in my life. I realized that in the area of marriage, my time had not yet come. I went back to the career change, then to the school thing again, all to no avail. I decided to ask the Lord what was the problem. He told me again, I needed to wait. He told me that He had plans for me to prosper and not to worry, He would give me hope and a future. We discussed my life and all that had occurred in it, my frustrations, disappointments, trials, and tribulations. I came to understand that everything in my life happened at a time in which it was destined to happen. My pastor always asks us the question, "Is it coincidence or providence?" Well, it was no coincidence that a broken heart brought me to Atlanta.

It was no coincidence, that the job that I absolutely did not

want, has become the best career move in my life. It is divine providence that I am at this particular station in life. Like Solomon said, "There is a season and a time to every purpose." We cannot rush our lives, we must live each day trusting in the Lord and waiting on Him. We must seek Him in every aspect of our lives in order that we might fulfill our purpose.

Patience is an attribute that does not come easy. In order to perfect our patience, we must endure the trials. We can run but we can never hide. We must learn the lesson that awaits us in order to move us on to the next phase. I am not suggesting that we sit back and do nothing. Developing patience is hard work. Remember the old saying, "A diamond is a piece of coal that stuck to the job." Never give up, no matter how difficult the road may be. Look to the Lord, He knows what you need and when you need it. Spend time in prayer and devotion. Rejoice in the blessings that you do have. Look to God above, seek Him and His will. Learn to serve others. Put self aside for a while in order that God may use you in order to fulfill His intended purpose for your life. Sometimes, we learn our lessons early, sometimes we learn them late. The important thing is that we learn life's lessons. Remember the lump of coal, and all that it went through in order that it might become a treasured possession. Seek God, trust God, wait on God. He will move in His own timing. After the grass grows, the cow will eat the grass, then, the cow gives milk.

Sharon Williams
Lithonia, GA

"A Lesson In 'Greatness'"

s I watched the reruns of the funeral processional and service of Princess Diana, Princess of Wales, I found myself looking up to Heaven and saying, "God, with all the good works this Lady had done, I sure hope her soul is in the Kingdom (the Kingdom of God that is).

All of a sudden, I got the bright idea that if I wanted to know if she was in the Kingdom all I had to do was ask the Holy Spirit. Before I could form the question in my mind. The Spirit of God answered in a very gentle voice and said "You don't need to Know." He was right. At that point there was nothing I could do, I have no Heaven or Hell to welcome her to.

But, the Spirit of God did not leave me ignorant in this matter. He taught me a great lesson in Greatness and Servanthood. He contrasted, for me, the events of this past week, in the death of two great women Princess Diana and Mother Teresa. I don't use the word "Great" lightly. In Matthew 20:26 & 27 (New King James version) Jesus said to his disciples "...whoever desires to become great among you, let him be your servant. And whoever desires to be first among you, let him be your slave..." Paraphrase: If you want to be great, be a servant. If you want to be greatest of the great, become a slave. Servants, these two great women, Mother Teresa and Princess Diana, Princess of Wales were, because of their capacity to LOVE people.

These great ladies are the twentieth century examples to the world of Matthew 20:27.

If ever there was a time God spoke simultaneously to the whole world, it was through the lives and death of these two women. If you missed the lesson in their life, let us not forget the lesson in their death. He who has ears let him hear what the Spirit of God is saying. God's excellence in Timing.

Had the death of these great ladies occurred in reverse order the impact would not have been as great. Mother Teresa's death would have been overshadowed by the death of Princess Diana. Look at God's impeccable timing! Just as we tried to pick ourselves up off the floor and regain our equilibrium, because of the violent jolt of Princess Diana's death we were reeling again because God plucked another Rose.

No one would have been very surprised at Mother Teresa's death because of her age. Heaven knows many of us have admired her. We have followed her ministry, and the news reports of her grave illness in past years. Some of us may have even whispered a prayer for her. But the death of Princess Diana, the English Rose, cut down in the middle of life, (we are promised 70 years). What a gut-wrenching shock. The tragic events of the last week was a wake up call to potential servants. It caused everyone "who has an ear to take stock of there own life and mortality." Human Greatness comes in all kinds of packages.

You don't have to be "rich" to be great, Mother Teresa certainly was not "rich." You don't have to be "poor" to be great,

Princes Diana was not "poor." You don't have to be "young" to be great, Mother Teresa was not "young." You don't have to be "old" to be great, Diana was not "old." You don't have to be "beautiful" to be great, Mother Teresa was not... well, I hope you get the picture. In my humble opinion, neither of these ladies could have done what they did without knowing the true God, in some capacity. Thank God, He did not take many of us by the time we were 36; need I say more.

In conclusion, the bottom line is this. There is no reason why we cannot be servants or great servants. All of our gifts, talents, and skills fall somewhere between the range of these two great women. If you want to be great, be a servant. If you want to be the greatest of the greats, become a slave. To be a slave of the people, it must come from the heart. From the heart flows the issues of life that move us into destiny and purpose or keep us out of it. We can only endure the obstacles and tests, if we are in destiny and purpose. These ladies lived destiny and in the end, they were honored in death by the world they served in life.

How does one know if he or she is in destiny and purpose, you may ask? Would you do what you do for free, week after week, month after month, year after year? If your answer is "yes" congratulations you're there!!!

Minister Virginia Richards
British Columbia, Canada

Drop The Baggage And
Move Forward

$\mathcal{I}$t is so easy to tell others how to handle and solve their issues and not follow the advice yourself. It was the early 90's and I was teaching a class that dealt with emotional baggage. As I listened to the stories participants shared, there were tears of joy, sorrow, and pain. At least, they had the courage to face the emotional scars impacting their lives. Now that they were sharing their stories, the release of pain was out. They could move forward. I sat there thinking about the one area of my life, I had not reconciled. I had rationalized that it did not matter. Who needs him, anyway? I had to ask myself, why am I wrestling with this issue? The person I am talking about is my father.

Since my parents had divorced when I was very young, a close relationship with my father did not exist. Growing up, I said it didn't matter. As an adult, I said the same thing. But in my heart, I knew it did. It hit home, while I was home in Indiana attending my aunt's funeral. I started to think how many people would love to have a father they could walk and talk with. I had cut off any ties with him

for many years. It's amazing how the death of a loved one, gets you to do some serious soul-searching. As I walked out of the cemetery, God was speaking to my heart. "You must change this situation." I felt so hypocritical. I had been teaching people how to face the very thing I had not been willing to face and change in my own life. Yes, I felt I had rationalized it intellectually, and had valid reasons for why it did not matter. But, it did matter. As I walked over to my father, the little voice in my head almost talked me out of making the contact. I told him we needed to talk, and resolve some issues. I asked him if we could go to dinner tonight? He lit up and responded with a quick yes. I got in my car and said to myself, "What have you done? Why are you rocking the boat?"

As I drove over to my mother's, I contemplated canceling the dinner meeting when I got home. It was the easy way out, but my spirit was saying "GO." I can't tell you the battle I faced in those few hours before our meeting. After so many years, what would be accomplished? In my heart I knew I wanted a relationship with my father. I felt like it was a second chance. Driving to the restaurant, I had an overwhelming desire to retreat and say "forget it." I reminded myself that it was time to practice what I had been preaching to others. My father was waiting as I entered the restaurant with a big smile. For me, it was awkward. Do you hug him, shake hands or what? I resolved to say hello and keep it safe. We sat down to dinner and made small talk. Finally, being the direct person I am, I dropped the baggage and let my feelings and emotions out. Release of the hurt, anger, and resentment came out as I struggled to understand the

past. My father, the direct man that he is, was honest and open about the past and answered my questions. I loosened up as I learned more about this man, my father. I saw the pain in his eyes for the history we had missed and could not reclaim. But we did have the future. The tension was now gone and we were laughing, as the bonding of a father and daughter had begun. It had been so easy, once I made up mind that the healing process had to begin. We began to have constant communication and more frank discussions. My father and I had so much in common. We could now learn even more about our commonalities. It was a great feeling. I left the restaurant many pounds lighter, because I let that baggage go. I reflected briefly on the years that had been wasted because of holding on to baggage that needed to be dropped. I say to those who are struggling with emotions with loved ones in your life, let it go. Don't waste precious time holding on to resentment, pain, and unforgiveness. It's unhealthy. I can say that my life has improved greatly since I made that step many years ago. It was a release of something that was on the way to becoming toxic. Today, I have a great relationship with my father, my friend. Remember, unforgiveness is unhealthy and forgiveness cleanses the soul. I knew in my heart what I needed to do. I finally submitted and let go, and let God direct my path. When we let God direct our steps, we are always victorious. I am grateful to God for a new beginning with my father.

Nancy J. Lewis, MS, PHR
Fayetteville, GA

Authors

Nancy J. Lewis is a business professional with over 15 years experience in training. Nancy has coached senior executives and their counterparts on a variety of issues. She has a masters degree in Urban and Public Affairs with concentration in Human Resources from Georgia State University.

Nancy delivers high energy during her motivational and informative seminars. She captivates the audience with her professional style. Therefore, you gain practical knowledge that immediately moves you toward greater achievement in life!! Ideas and effective techniques shared in Nancy's seminars provide necessary tools for transforming your life. Her areas of expertise include customer service, communication skills, managing change, leadership, and inspirational/motivational keynotes.

Nancy is the president of Progressive Techniques, Inc. where the theme of her company is "Developing a Better You!" The mission statement of Progressive Techniques, Inc. is "Changing the world, one person at a time." Nancy is the author of *Things To Do To Be A Better You!* She is the co-author of *Sisters Together: The Best Quotes We Have Heard, Said, or Read, That Have Anchored Our Souls* and *Sisters Together: Lessons Learned That Have Anchored Our Souls.*

You can reach Nancy at: Progressive Techniques, Inc.
P.O. Box 342
Fayetteville, GA 30214
Phone: 404-559-7614
Fax: 770-306-8237
email: nancyjlewis@bellsouth.net
website: http://www.nancyjlewis.com

Authors

Debra Washington Gould is an inspirational speaker, management consultant, and trainer based in New Orleans, LA.. An experienced workshop leader who specializes in self development seminars in leadership, interpersonal, organizational, goal setting, and time management skills. Debra earned an Master's of Science Degree in Management from Florida Institute of Technology and received a Bachelor of Science Degree in Accounting from Southern University at New Orleans.

She is a co-author of the *Sisters Together* series, *The Best Quotes We Have Heard, Read or Said That Have Anchored Our Souls* and *Sisters Together: Lessons Learned That Have Anchored Our Souls.*

Debra, a native of New Orleans, is also *an enthusiastic professional speaker who speaks from the heart.* Debra is happily married to Joseph Gould, Jr. and the proud mother of Joseph Gould, III. Debra gives her audiences the tools to Inspire, Motivate, and Grow! You can reach Debra at:

P. O. Box 871211
New Orleans, Louisiana 70187-1211
phone: (504)244-6576 or toll free:(800)699-8091
fax: (504)243-2058
email:djgould@gouldassoc.com
website: http://www.gouldassoc.com

"Persistence Beats Resistance Every Time"

Contributors

Tereska Bridges Washington, RN (*Finally, We Meet, pp.71*), of New Orleans, LA, is the loving wife of Tyrone Washington, Sr. and the caring mother of their son, Tyrone, Jr. She is a registered nurse at the Medical Center of Louisiana at New Orleans. An avid student of the Bible, Tereska attends Deliverance Temple Church of God In Christ where she teaches the adult Sunday School class. A favorite Bible verse that anchors her soul is *I can do all things through Christ which strengthenth me.* (Philippians 4: 13)

Pamela Sherrard, ODC/MS (*Piercing The Armour, pp.143*) is a daughter, mother, mother-in-law, grandmother, and veteran employee of the Federal Court System. Involved for many years in reconstruction and design of her life towards peace and ambition, Pamela is a certified ontological coach and a movement psychologist.

Cynthia Curry Crim (*Don't Look Back, pp. 23*) is Assistant Director of the Ounce of Prevention Fund's O-5 Head Start Program in Chicago. She is a graduate of Southern University,(B.A., Political Science), and Atlanta University, (M.A.,Pub. Admin.). Cynthia is married and enjoys walking, eating out, sailing and reading.

Sharyn Scheyd (*Just Say Yes! pp. 128*) is president of Sharyn Scheyd, Inc. a personal and professional development company and a member of the National Speakers Association. She speaks regularly on celebrating our gifts and reaching our potential. She lives in Kenner, LA with her three children. Contact Sharyn Scheyd, Inc., P.O. Box 641642, Kenner, LA 70064.

Arlene LeBlanc Broussard (*Good Fortune, pp.124*) is a double Cajun, who enjoys life to the fullest. She owns SpeakerSource, a full service speakers bureau. Arlene works with groups that want dynamic presentations, and with meeting planners that want the right speakers. Contact Arlene at SpeakerSource, 112 Cane Drive, Lafayette, LA, 70508-4312. Phone: (318)-236-3714, 1-(888)-363-4180 (toll free) or ssource@bellsouth.net.

Contributors

Monica Pierre (*"Mirror, Mirror" pp.68*) is an Emmy Award-winning television journalist, radio personality, author and professional speaker. Monica is founder of the Pierre Principle, a motivational and public seminar company. In her newly-released book of motivation, *Found My Soul In A Sweet Potato Patch - Living A Life of Victory,* Monica has created a sweet formula for success.

Carole Copeland Thomas, MBA *(An Open Letter To My Dear Friends, pp.49)* is a lecturer and trainer who specializes in leadership development, empowerment and diversity. She is a member of the National Speakers Association and lives in Woburn, MA. For information, contact, C. Thomas and Associates, 400 W. Cummings Park, #1725-154, Woburn, MA 08101. (617) 938-5502 or 1-800-801-6599.

Sandra S. Dawson *(My Daughter's Spiritual Healing, pp. 52)* is a PC Support Specialist for the Strategic Petroleum Reserve, Department of Energy. She is president of Dawson Trucking of LaPlace Louisiana. Sandra still spends quality time at Church and at home, along with her husband, raising two daughters and a son.

Tom Ella McBeth (*Shedding My Earth Suit, pp. 84*) is a Human Resources professional and trainer. She is also president of the Job Coalition Network Assocation, Inc. Tom Ella is a woman who is about continuous improvement to be the best she can be. She is a resident of Riverdale, GA where she lives with her son.

Sharon Williams *(Before The Grass Becomes Milk, pp.166)* is a Medical Technologist who lives in Lithonia, GA. A model of devotion to her spiritual beliefs, Sharon is always willing to help others and is very active in her church and community.

Contributors

Wanda Anderson Davis, Esq. *(Coming Face To Face With Self, pp.54)* is an attorney in the private practice of law, a hearing officer for the Louisiana State Bar Association, and an entrepreneur. She also holds leadership positions in many professional and civic organizations.

Patricia Munford *(From Rags To Riches, pp. 91)* is an administrative assistant for the Fulton County Public Schools. She is very active in her Church and community. She makes her home in College Park, GA where she raises her three beautiful daughters.

C. Arnold *("When Life Deals You A Lemon..." pp. 160)* is a concerned and committed wife and mother who shares the joy of raising a beautiful daughter with her husband Norris. She enjoys an involved church life and participates in the betterment of her community of College Park, GA.

Willie R. Haywood *(The Reunion, pp.157)* is the owner of Outlook on Health Communications, Inc. She is publisher of *Outlook On Health* a magazine and author of *When The Shoes Fit,* a book on the issue of domestic violence. Ms. Haywood is a former nurse and received a B.A. in Health Education from The Union Institute. She also attended the University of Cincinnati's Graduate Program in Health Education.

Abby Shields, MEd *(Lessons From A Three Year Old, pp. 97)* is a dynamic international speaker and author who has the ability to bring objectivity, sensitivity, enthusiasm, and a liberal dose of humor to her programs. Shields is author of *"Little Bits of Wisdom"* a book of survival skills for teenagers and their parents. She is also a newspaper columnist for two newspapers.

Contributors

Thelma L. Wells, *(Foreword, pp.vii.)* is CEO of Thelma Wells &Associates. She is a nationally known public speaker and author. She is the author of *Bumblebees Fly Anyway; Defying the Odds at Work and Home* and the soon-to-be released *God Will Make A Way.* Since 1984, she has been serving some of the nation's top corporations and community groups. Ms. Wells is married and has three children.

A.A.G., *(Saved My Life, pp. 21)* is a wife and mother of one son Gilbert. She makes her home in New Orleans, LA. She owns her own business, is involved in the community and spends time with her son.

Sheree T. Venson-Nelson, *(Then and Now, pp. 139)* is a graduate of Southern University of Baton Rouge where she obtained a B.S. in Psychology and an A.S. in Law Enforcement. She currently works as unit coordinator for the General Clinic Research Center at Tulane University. She is a member of the New Home Full Gospel Ministries and enjoys quality time with her husband Michael and son Zhane.

Mary Kay Kurzweg, *(Order That Pizza, pp. 151)* is an award winning international speaker who has trained a host of executives to speak with style and grace. Her seminar topics cover a broad range of topics, but all include having *fun*! For more information contact: MKK & Co., 215 Stella St., Metairie, LA 70005, 800-493-2983, MKKurzweg@aol.com.

Minister Virginia Richards, *(A Lesson In Greatness, pp.170),* is a licensed, ordained minister of the Gospel with the Full Gospel Ministry. She's presently serving in British Columbia, Canada.

Contributors

Barbara J. Cypher, MEd *(Family Values and Math: A Study of Probability, pp.135)* holds an M. Ed., and a Bachelor of Science in Elementary education from the United States. She has taught 1st, 4th, and 5th grades, ESL, and Reading in the USA and internationally for over sixteen years. She can be contacted by e-mail at 105070.1456@compuserve.com.

Twanda Black *(Why Me? - One of Life's Important Lessons, pp.94)* is Public Affairs Director for Jazz Flavors104.1 FM in Atlanta. The College Park, GA resident is the mother of two sons, who are her joy as is the sharing of the Gospel. Twanda is also a licensed ordained minister.

Carol Pierce MEd *(Thank You, Nicole! pp.25)* is an author, professional speaker, human relations consultant, and trainer. In an energetic, fast-paced style, she reveals to her audiences how to overcome obstacles in their lives. She further discusses this topic in her forthcoming book, *Jump Now, Look Later: New Ways to Beat Old Fears*. She resides in South Louisiana and has three children.

Evelyn Davis Williams *("You Must Be Better Than The Best, To Get Half of The Rest," pp.36)* is the wife of John Howard Williams. They are natives of Knoxville, Tennessee. Evelyn retired from Knoxville City School System in 1981 where she was an elementary principal. She is also lifetime member Alpha Kappa Alpha Sorority.

Judy Moon Denson *(Life is a Dance! pp.107)* is a professional speaker and author who makes her home in Hattiesburg, MS. Her latest book is titled *KidSpiration ... Out of the Mouths of Babes*.

Contributors

Shirley Lundy-Connor, MEd *(The Christmas Present, pp. 41)* COE Foundation for Living-has dedicated her life to helping clients confront, accept and overcome the obstacles in their lives. Her work has allowed her to serve several special needs groups including chemically dependent adults and their children, survivors of sexual/physical abuse, learning disabled, emotionally disturbed and physically challenged children.

Akua Wambui (a.k.a Carol Bebelle), *(Simple Things Remind Me, pp.101)* is a native New Orleanian. She received her undergraduate degree (BA) from Loyola University in Sociology and her Master's Degree (M.Ed) from Tulane University in Education Administration. She is president of Master Plan Development Associates (MPDA), a private consultant firm that provides planning, development and grant writing services. You may contact her at : AKUA Productions, Inc., 1029 Hillary Street, New Orleans, LA 70118. (504) 861-4969 / FAX (504) 866-6084.

Patricia Crawford, *(Love Thy Neighbor, pp. 46)* is a graduate of McNeese State University, Lake Charles, LA. Patricia is a Configuration Management Specialist from Baton Rouge, LA. where she is very active in her church and community. She is married and has one daughter.

Yolanda E. Scott, MSW *(My Lesson in Faith, pp.73)* is a supervisor with an agency that treats pregnant and post-partum substance abusing mothers and their family. Having a strong relationship with God, Yolanda is committed to sharing the glow of this experience as well as her professional training to inspire others to make a difference in their life.

Contributors

Veronica Toussaint White (*Sleepless Nights, pp. 38*) is an entrepreneur and successful owner of Shear Magic Hair Salon. She earned a Bachelor of Science Degree in Public Health at Dillard University in New Orleans, LA. She is presently working on a Master's in Environmental Health Sciences at Tulane University School of Public Health. She lives in New Orleans, Louisiana with her husband David and her daughter Jasmine.

Marion Wikholm MSW, BCSW, (*With Bullets of Determination, pp.146*) is a Polio survivor, who works with people who want to feel great about themselves, and with organizations that want to help employees develop a positive attitude. Marion is a professional psychotherapist, speaker, and humorist. She's developed a unique formula for becoming a better person by mixing humor with a sizable portion of psychological insights in her book entitled: *Bitter or Better; It's Up to You.*

Barbara A. Eveque-Hornsby, CPA, (*Grief & Strength, pp. 131*) an accounting graduate of Loyola University. She has been employed five years by the United States Department of Agriculture Office of Inspector General Office as an auditor. Also, she has owned and operated an Accounting and Tax practice for the past eight years.

Lois Gould-Ford (*Coping, pp.125* and *I Understand, pp.126*) is a Southern University, New Orleans graduate, an Internal Audit Manager for a local utility company. A City Certified Manager. Mother of two and "a young" grandmother of two. A novice bible study teacher. She enjoys gardening, art and intelligent conversation.

Contributors

Greta D. Jefferson, *(Overcoming Adversity, pp.164)* is a native of New Orleans who has a strong spiritual relationship and appreciates the value of family and good friends. An active community leader, she shares her gifts to the benefit of those in need of assistance.

Frances Marie Smith-Dean, *(Overcoming Adversity Through Christ, pp. 58)* is a Mathematics Instructor and Coordinator of the New Orleans Public Schools MONEY MATTER$ PROGRAM. A graduate of Xavier University of LA, (BS in Computer Science) and Loyola University, (MST in Mathematics), Ms. Smith-Dean is a dedicated teacher, administrator, and role-model in the sciences, in business as well as her spiritual walk. She is married to Darryl Dean and they have one daughter, Frances Mary.

Carmella Marshall, *(The Lesson of '95 - We're all doing the best we can do" pp. 63)* is a gospel and inspirational singer. A recording artist who has toured Europe, Carmella's been singing since childhood. In addition to recording two gospel albums, she's also recorded a French children's album. At the magnificent age of 40, she is a wife and mother who loves life and enjoys seeing her life unfold into new challenges and opportunities.

Durinda L. Robinson, *("Kick The Ladder Away, Live Your Dreams And Just Do It.," pp. 153)* is an attorney, actress, model, standup comic, and chief executive officer (CEO) of Cleopatra Foods. As CEO of Cleopatra Foods, she has developed along with a government scientist, a line of rice-based food products that are packaged and marketed in a growing number of stores. People with hypoglycemia, allergies, and glucose intolerance now have healthy snack alternatives in their diets. You can contact her at : Cleopatra Foods, 64 Grand Canyon Drive, New Orleans, LA 70131, (504) 392-6424.

Order Form

To order your copy of *Sisters Together: Lessons Learned That Have Anchored Our Souls* please submit your request with payment to either of the addresses listed below:

Debra Gould & Associates, LLC   or Progressive Techniques, Inc.
P.O. Box 8711211   P.O. Box 342
New Orleans, LA 70187-1211   Fayetteville, GA 30214

(Print or Type)

Name: _____

Address: _____

City: _____ State _____ zip _____

My order for *Sisters Together* is as follows:

_____Copies @ $14.95 per copy : _____

9% LA State Sales Tax ($1.35 ea.) _____

Shipping & Handling   ($3.50 ea.) _____

Total: _____

(Please make copies of this form)

Contributor Submission Request

You are invited to submit your story for publication in future editions of *Sisters Together.* We welcome your Lessons Learned story, that it may inspire others, as you become part of our growing sisterhood of contributors. Your story can be of simple yet profound truths that give life perspective and meaning, or of inspiring, thoughtful or life-changing experiences.

You can expect to be contacted within two weeks with instructions for submission. Please submit your request in writing to either author/address listed below.

Debra Washington Gould   Nancy J. Lewis
Debra Gould & Associates, LLC   or   Progressive Techniques, Inc.
P.O. Box 871211   P.O. Box 342
New Orleans, LA 70187-1211   Fayetteville, GA 30214

You may also request *Sisters Together: Lessons Learned That Have Anchored Our Souls* at your local book store by providing them with title and the ISBN number, **ISBN: 0-9660306-5-6.**